Anatomy

Originally, the fascinating study of m[...] scientific treatises. But during the Renaissance, there wa[...] Greek philosophy —the purity of the naked form and [...] particular focus in Western art, and a desire to learn abo[...] body meant that by the late sixteenth century, cadavers were released for dissection not only to physicians, but also to artists. This study of anatomy soon became institutionalized through art academies.

Although an in-depth scientific knowledge of anatomy is not necessary, an understanding of anatomy is crucial for competent depictions of the body in any visual medium and is also the fundamental basis by which you can develop your techniques toward portrait and figure drawing. This sketchbook is part of a series to help develop your drawing skills across different subjects, and in this book we include a selection of works that show human anatomy in a broad range of styles and media to copy from and be inspired by. These are accompanied by thoughts from commentators and the artists themselves, and there is also a general information section on materials and techniques for the beginner.

Drawing the human form is a constant challenge for any artist and you don't have to wait until you have the time to create a full-length work of a whole body—preparatory sketches, practice exercises, or even a few scribbles will go a long way to sharpening your observational skills and building up your knowledge of how the human body works. If you carry your sketchbook with you everywhere and practice drawing regularly, in time, this sketchbook will become a record of your progress and commitment to improving your skills.

Skeletons, anatomical models, medical specimens, and live nude models may not be available to many, but sketching in galleries, museums, or from books is an invaluable training tool. Indeed, Italian artists of the fifteenth century notably turned to classical masterpieces to copy from. In turn, the examples set by the great artists in this sketchbook will help you hone your drawing skills of proportion, foreshortening, rendering basic forms, and effective use of light and shade. As Damien Hirst (b.1965) said: "You've got to be able to copy things faithfully before you can deviate," and the aim of this book is to provide you with a good technical understanding that encourages you to create your own interpretations of the human body with a naturalness of form and expression, in your own style.

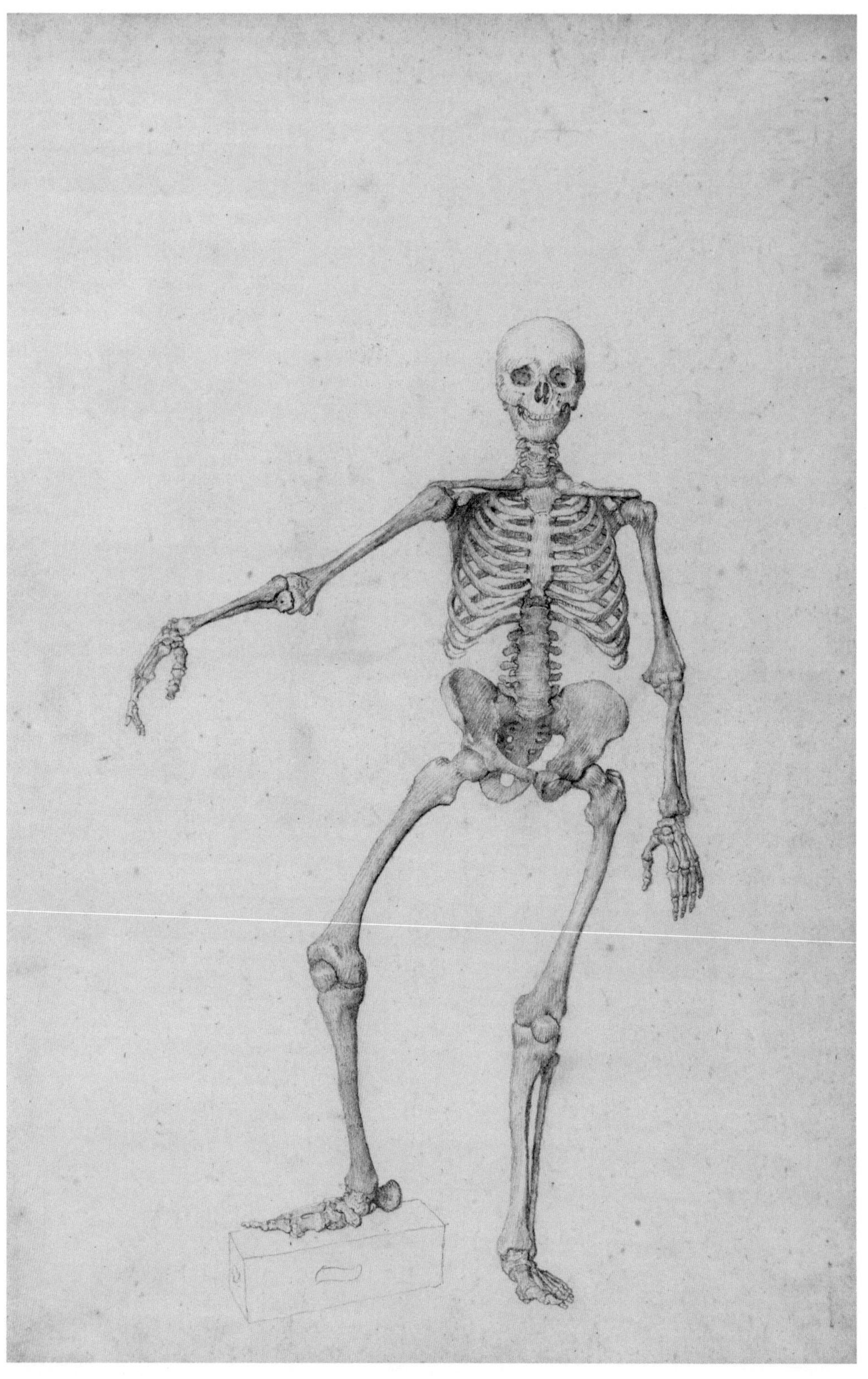

George Stubbs
(1724—1806)
HUMAN SKELETON,
ANTERIOR VIEW,
RIGHT ARM
OUTSTRETCHED
1795–1806
Graphite on thin
wove paper
Yale Center for British Art,
Paul Mellon Collection

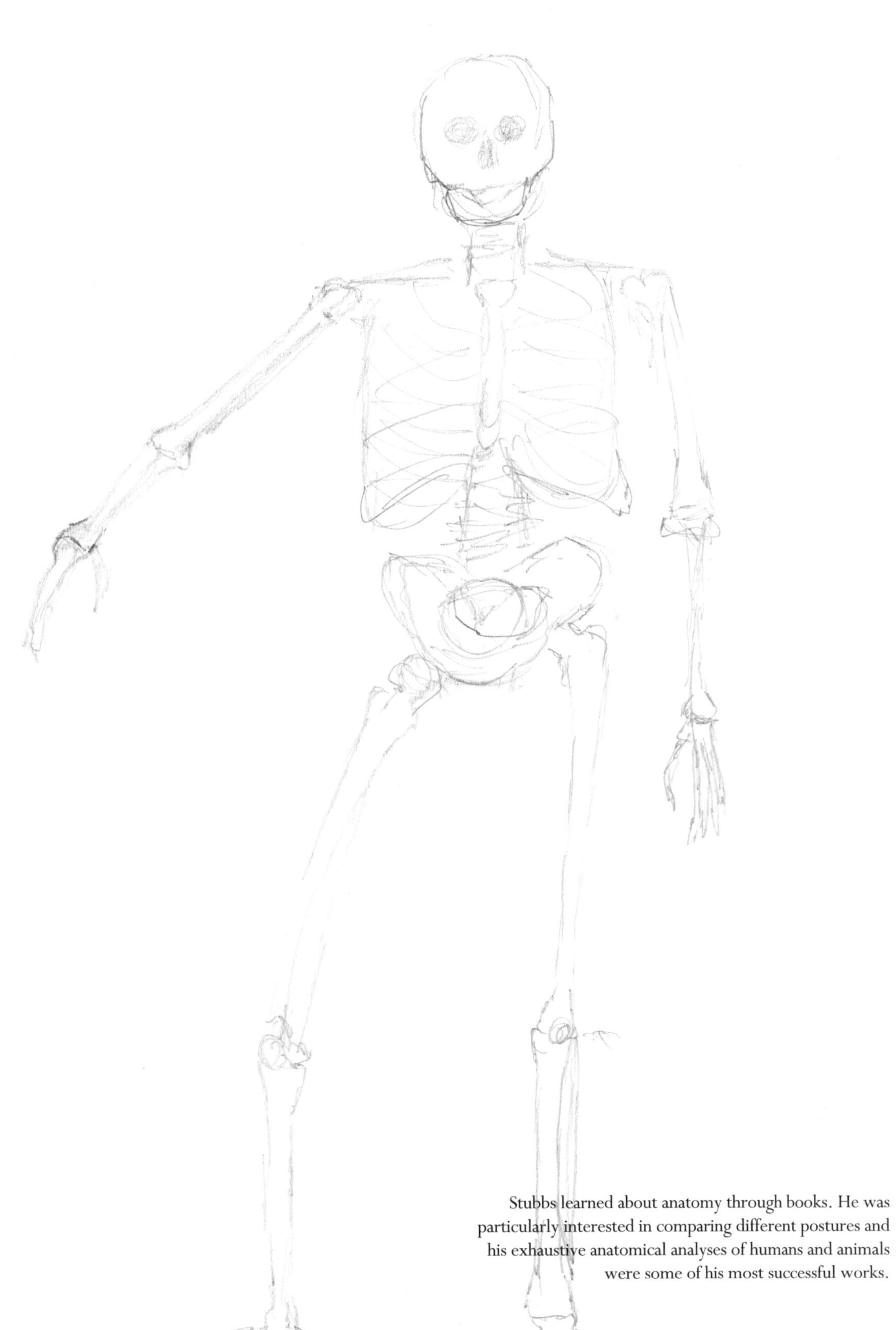

Stubbs learned about anatomy through books. He was
particularly interested in comparing different postures and
his exhaustive anatomical analyses of humans and animals
were some of his most successful works.

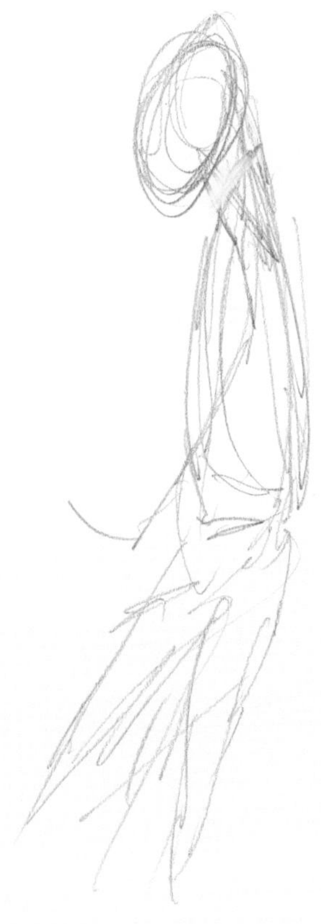

The skeleton acts as a framework for the body to hang onto and determines the pose of your sitter. It can be useful to make sketches of skeletons to gain a better understanding of how bodies move and their physical limitations.

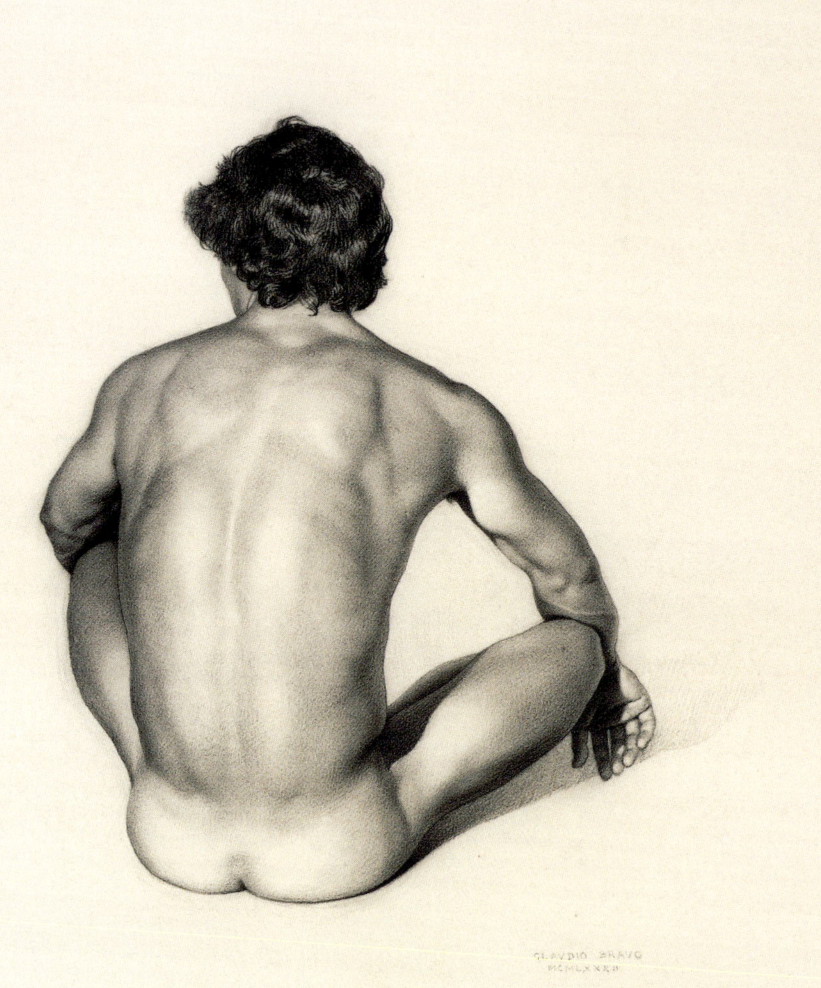

Claudio Bravo
(1936–2011)
SEATED
MALE NUDE
1982
Pencil and charcoal
on buff paper
*Private collection/Photo
Christie's Images/Bridgeman
Images © The Estate of
Claudio Bravo, courtesy
Marlborough Gallery,
New York*

Think of the back as an anchor for the body. The head, the rib cage, and the pelvis are all connected by the spine—draw these three masses as attachments along the central vertebral column and build the rest of the body around them.

*The photo-realists, like machines, copied directly
from photographs. Always I have relied on the actual subject
matter because the eye sees so much more than the camera:
half tones, shadows, minute changes in the color or light.*
CLAUDIO BRAVO

David d'Angers
(1788–1856)
HUMAN ANATOMY;
MUSCLES OF THE
TORSO AND
SHOULDER
19TH CENTURY
Pencil and red chalk
on paper
*Musée des Beaux-Arts,
Angers/Bridgeman Images*

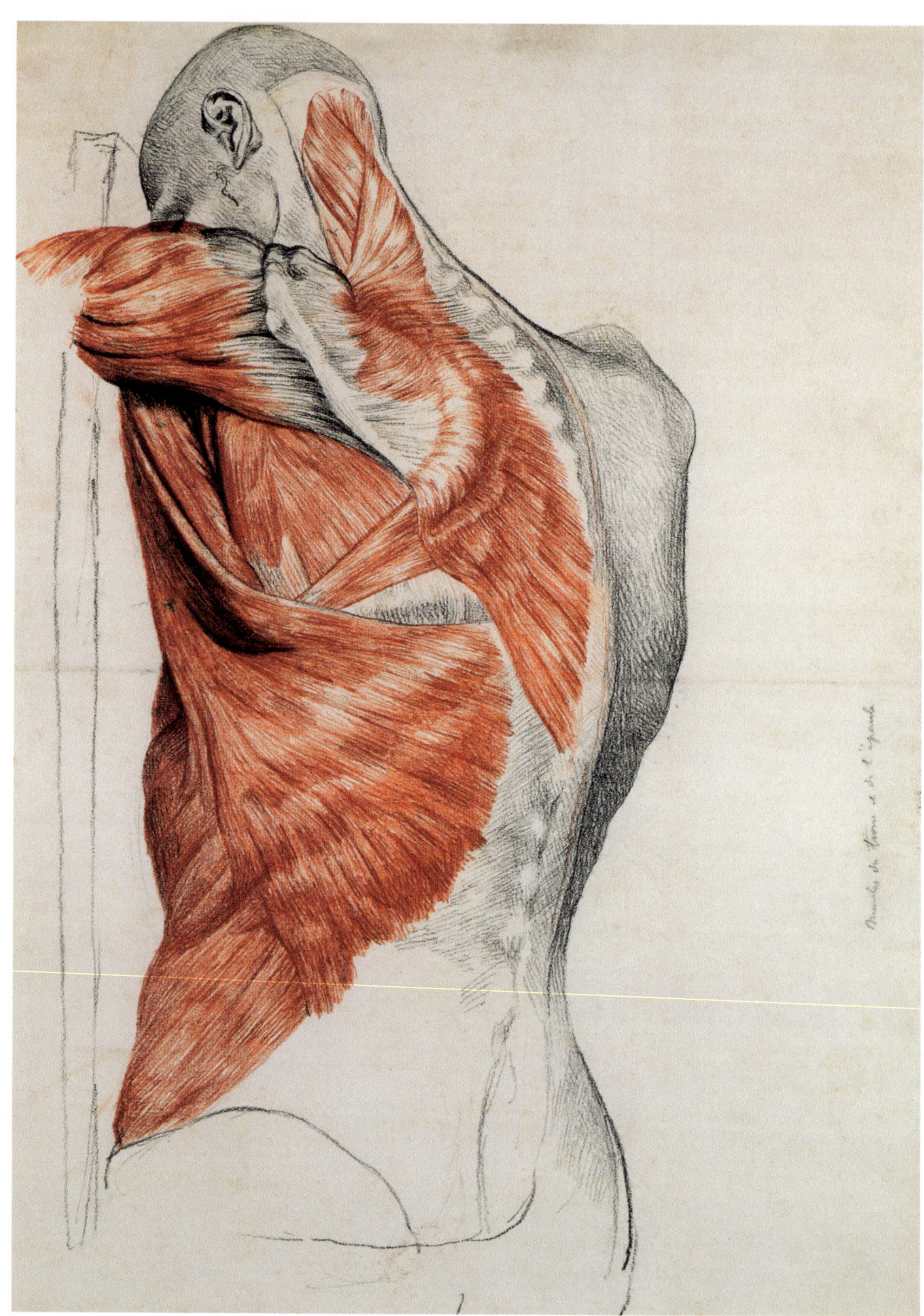

Écorché ("flayed") is an established conceit in art, particularly
in anatomical studies, whereby the body is depicted without skin.
In the sixteenth century these would have been circulated among
artists to further their study and understanding of human anatomy.

The function of muscle is to pull and not to push,
except in the case of the genitals and the tongue.
LEONARDO DA VINCI

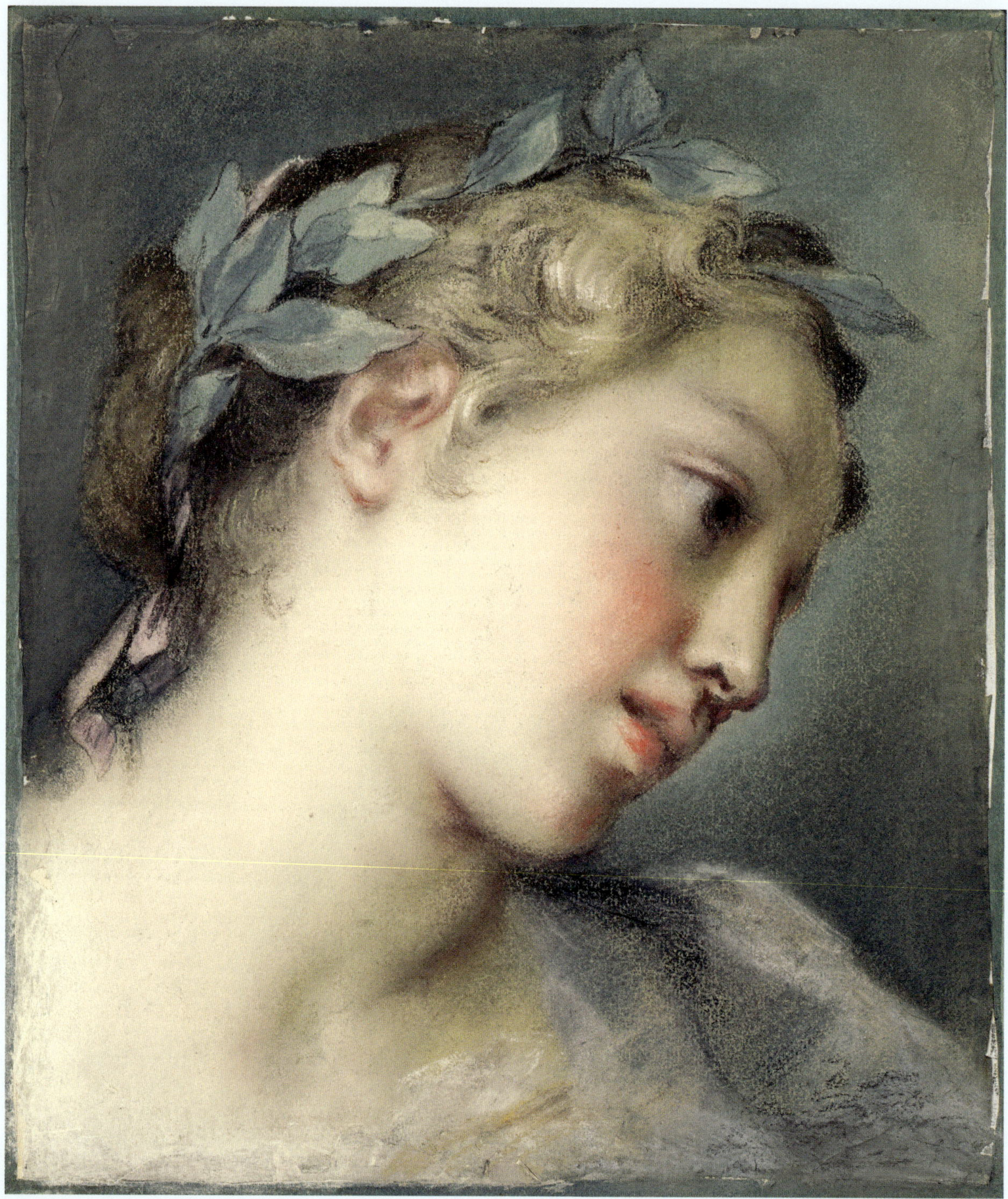

Rosalba Carriera
(1673–1757)
A MUSE
MID-1720S
Pastel on laid blue paper
*J. Paul Getty Museum,
California. Image courtesy
of the Getty's Open
Content Program*

The powdery softness of pastel makes it ideal for
drawing skin. It possesses a vibrant mid-tone that can be
easily modified to create a colorful yet subtle portrait
and edges can be blended for an ethereal effect.

*And your very flesh shall be a great poem and have the
richest fluency not only in its words but in the silent
lines of its lips and face and between the lashes of your
eyes and in every motion and joint of your body.*

WALT WHITMAN

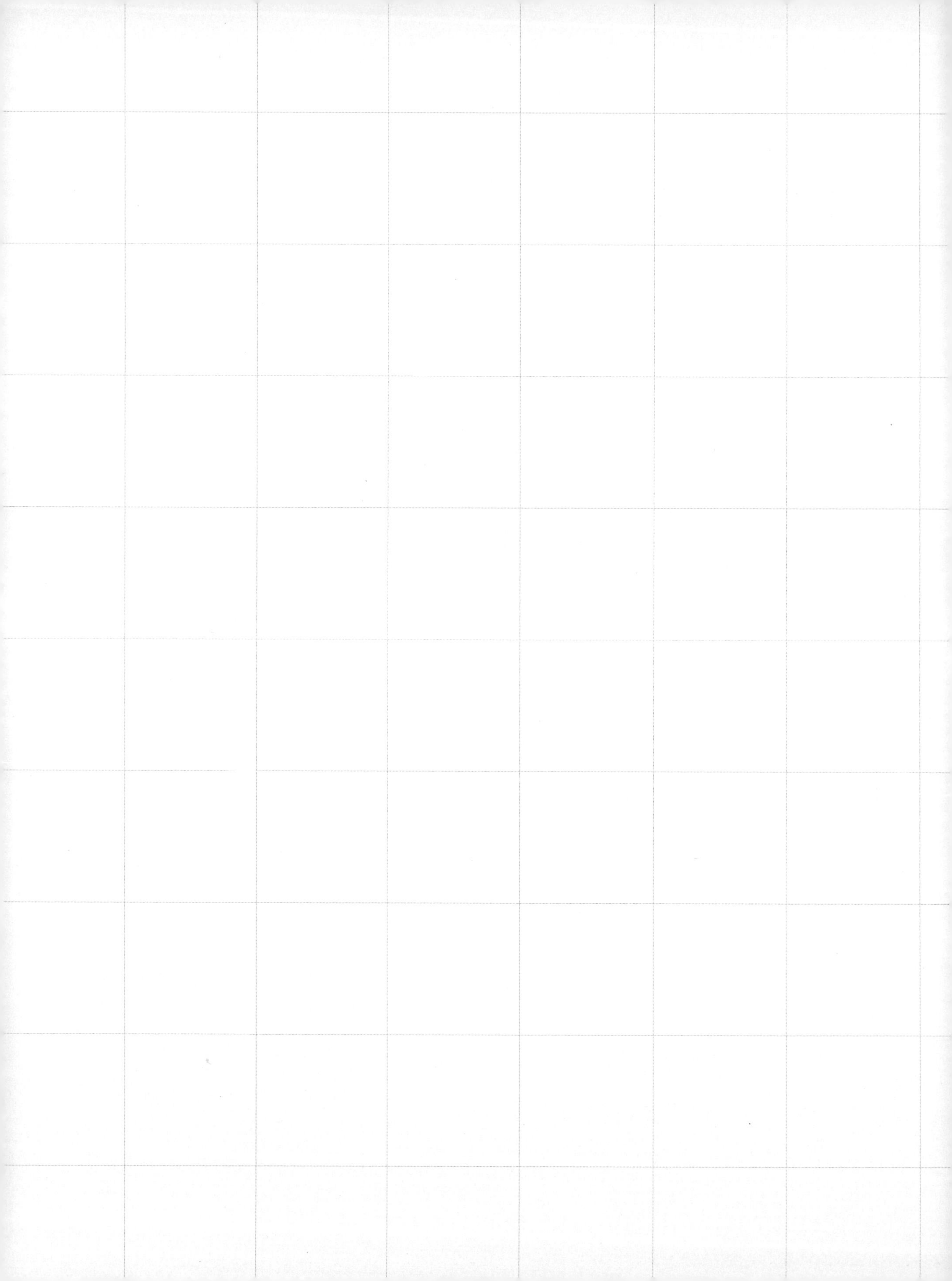

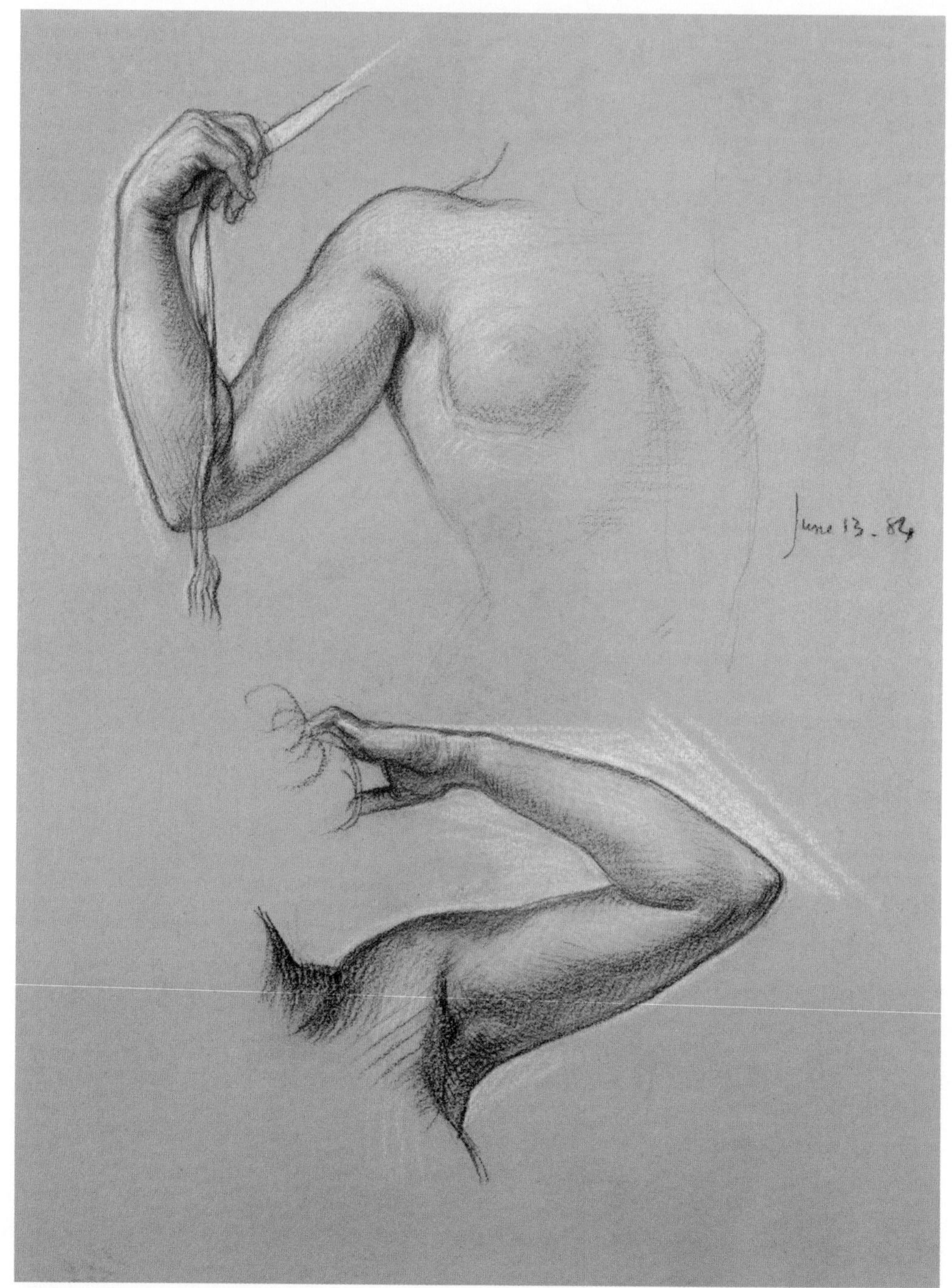

Edward Poynter
(1836–1919)
TWO STUDIES OF
THE SHOULDERS
AND RAISED ARMS
OF A GIRL FOR
DIADUMENE
1884
Chalk on paper
*Private Collection/
Photo Peter Nahum at
The Leicester Galleries,
London/Bridgeman Images*

The shoulder joint offers the greatest range of
motion in the body. The shoulder and hip joints
are ball and socket joints, which allow for a
rotation in almost all directions.

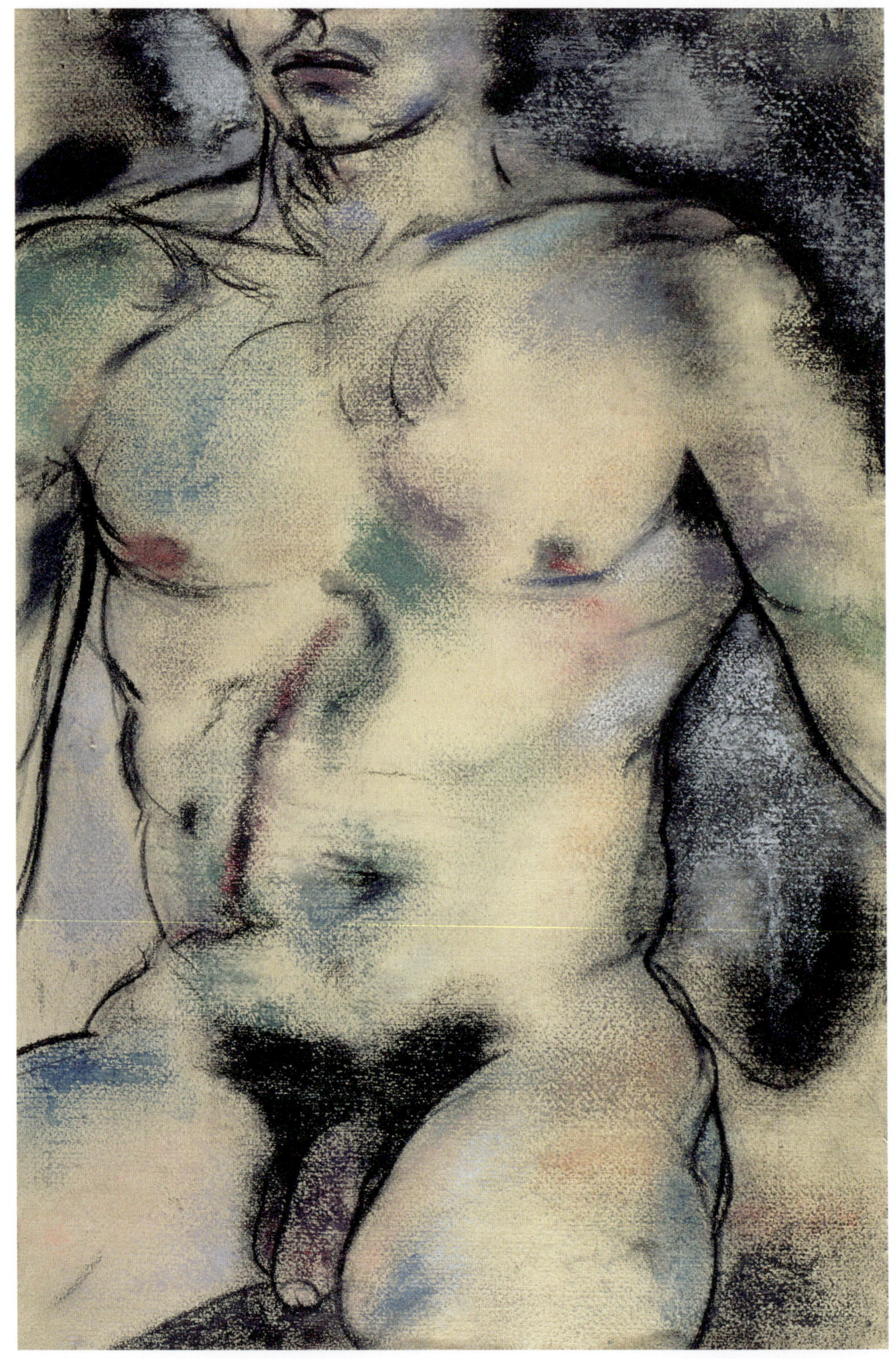

R. B. Kitaj
(1932–2007)
ACTOR (RICHARD)
1979
Pastel and charcoal
on paper
*National Galleries of
Scotland, Edinburgh/
Bridgeman Images*
© R. B. Kitaj Estate

Art has had many ideals through its history and the penis too has
had these imposed upon it. In ancient Egypt, circumcision is
evident in artworks; in ancient Greece and Rome, the phallus was
shown as small and uncircumcised generally; and in Edo-period
Japan, shunga works show exaggerated member sizes.

Genitalia are a symbol of fertility and erotica in art.
Consider if a rendition is idealized or not. What are the
colors and forms involved, and on what scale?

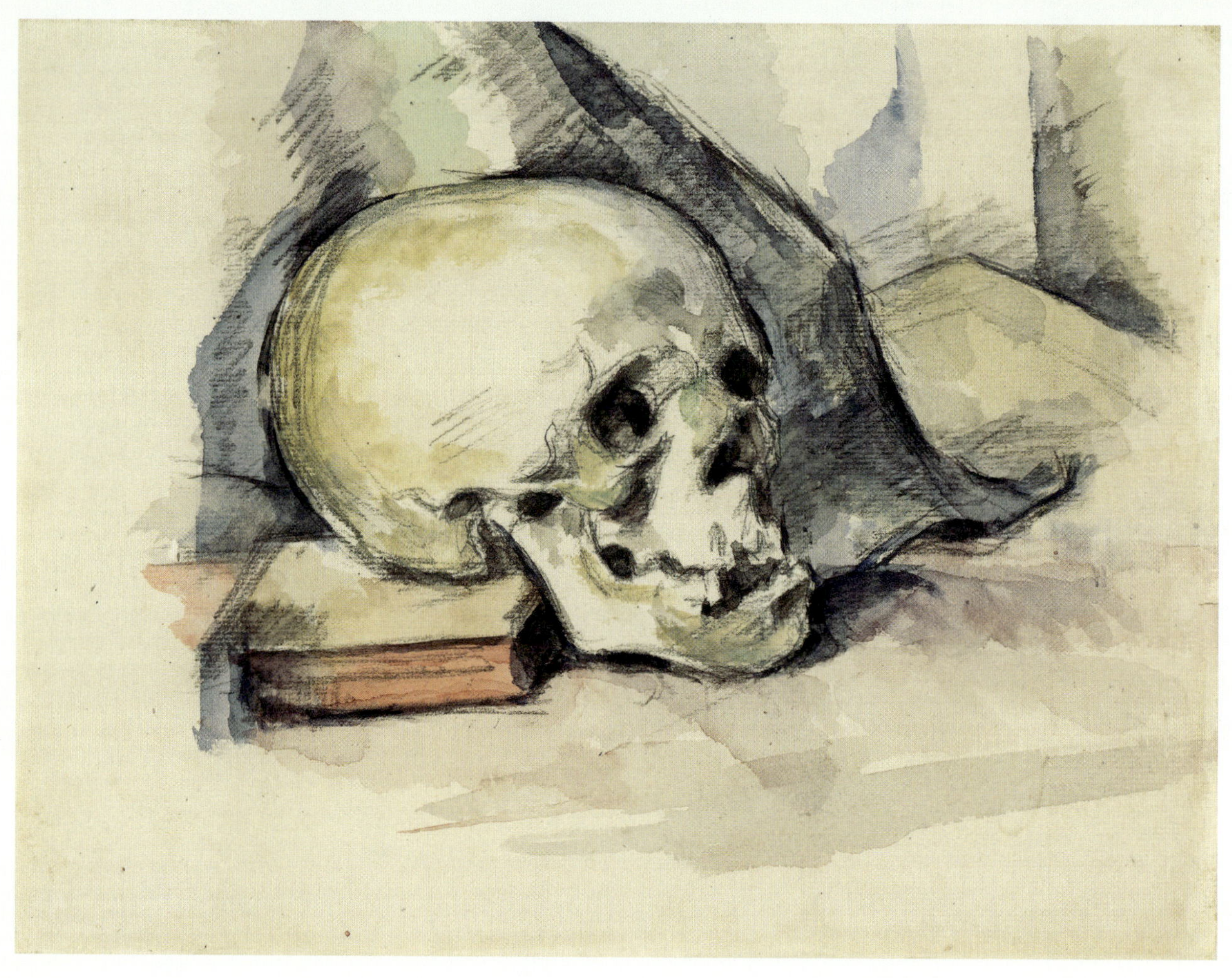

Paul Cézanne

(1839–1906)

SKULL AND BOOK

C.1885

Watercolor over
black chalk on paper

Destroit Institute of Arts.
Bequest of John S. Newberry/
Bridgeman Images

Memento mori are symbols of mortality, and the skull is often represented as one. The phrase "memento mori" means "remember what you have before you die," and this spiritual imperative holds a strong power that reminds people to live moral lives.

The skull is nature's sculpture.
DAVID BAILEY

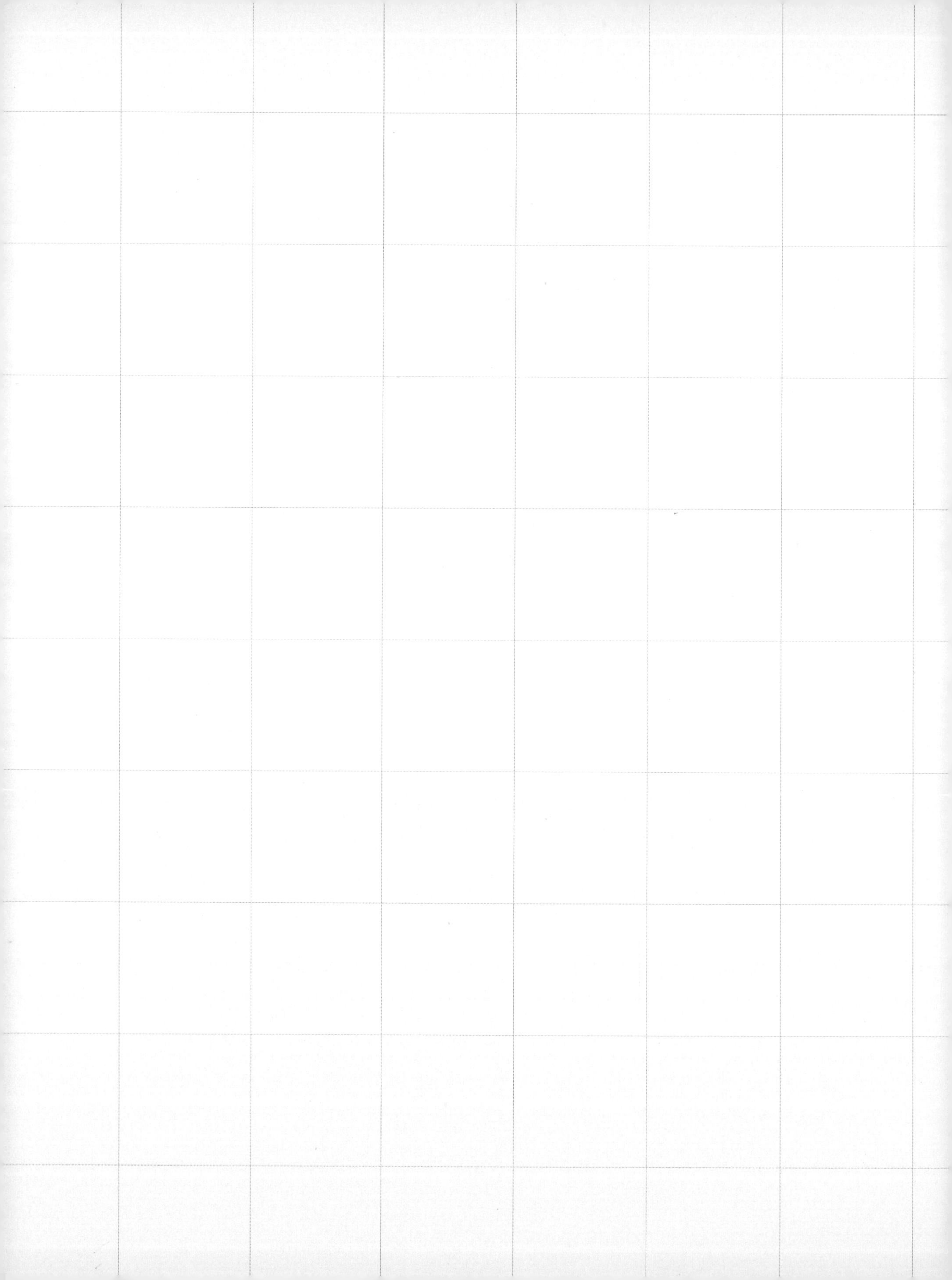

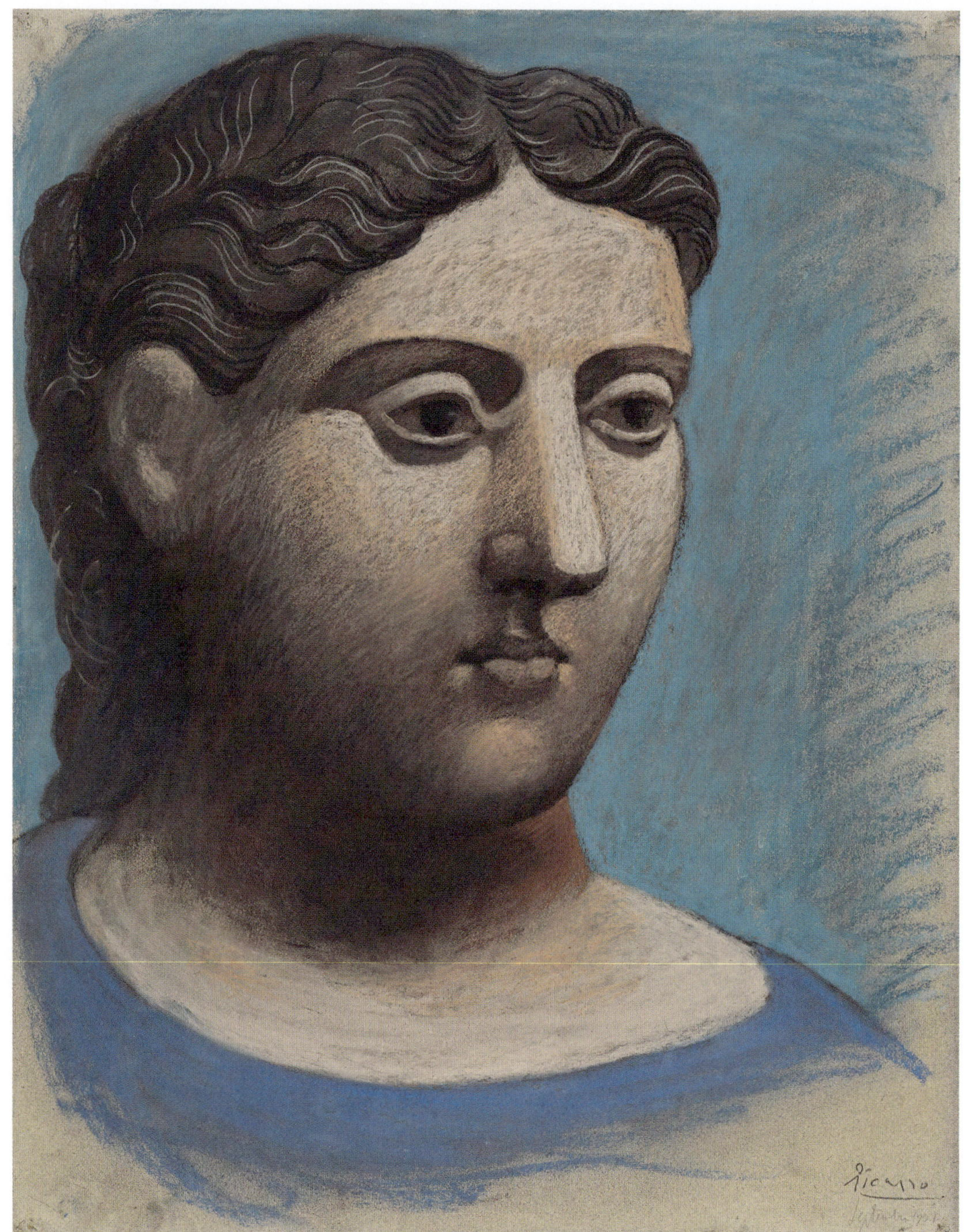

Pablo Picasso

(1881–1973)

HEAD OF A WOMAN

1921

Pastel on paper

*The Metropolitan Museum
of Art, New York. Bequest of
Scofield Thayer, 1982/Photo
The Metropolitan Museum
of Art/Art Resource/Scala,
Florence © Succession
Picasso/DACS, London 2018*

This piece was inspired by the ancient wall paintings Picasso visited in
Italy in 1917. The monumentality of the head is suggested through solid
forms and dramatic shading that give the drawing a sculptural feel.

Before drawing a head, establish the angle. Consider
the head as a ball on a pivot and roughly align the
various elements of the eyes, ears, nose, and mouth,
taking note of the head's proportional symmetry.

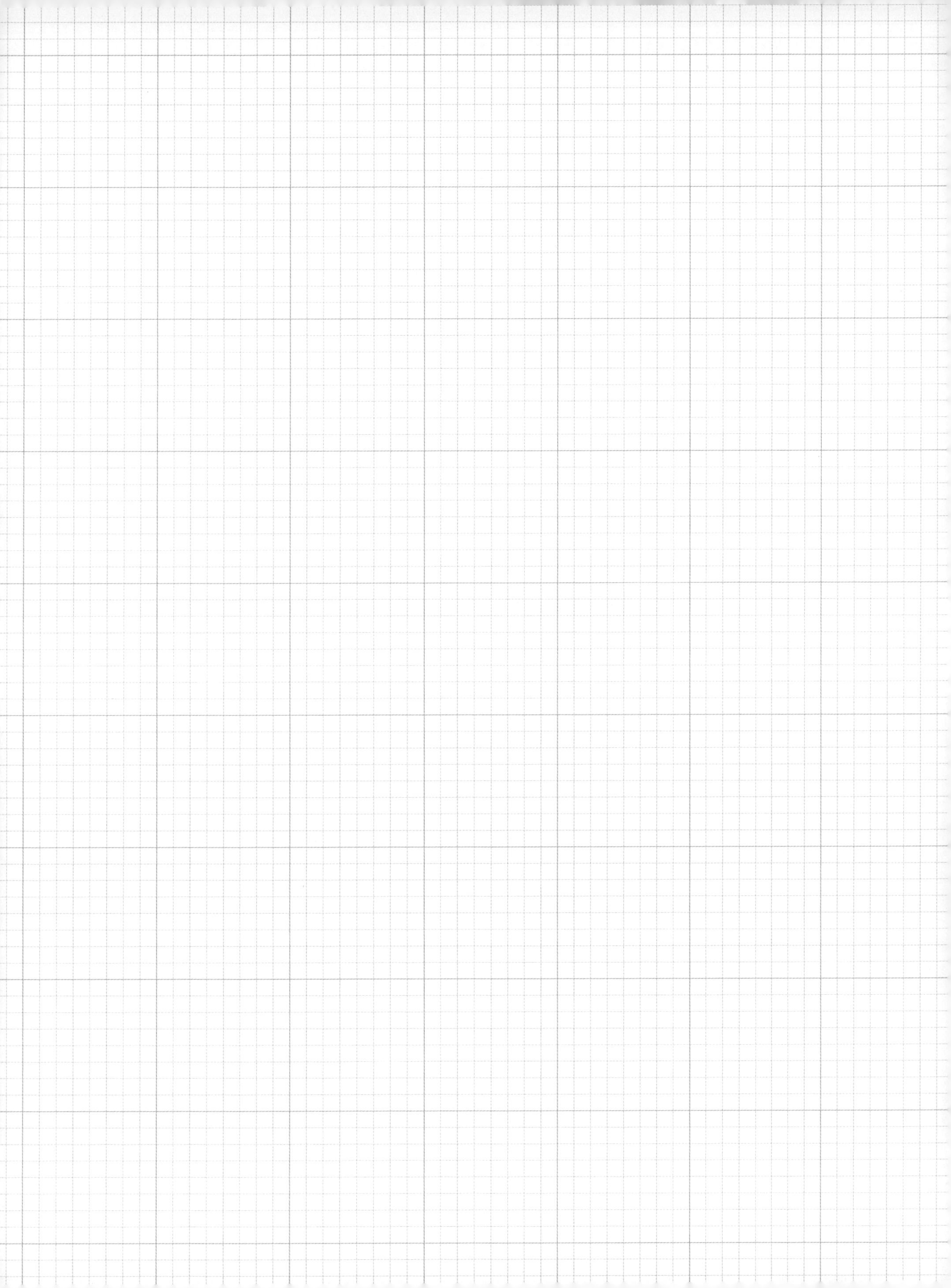

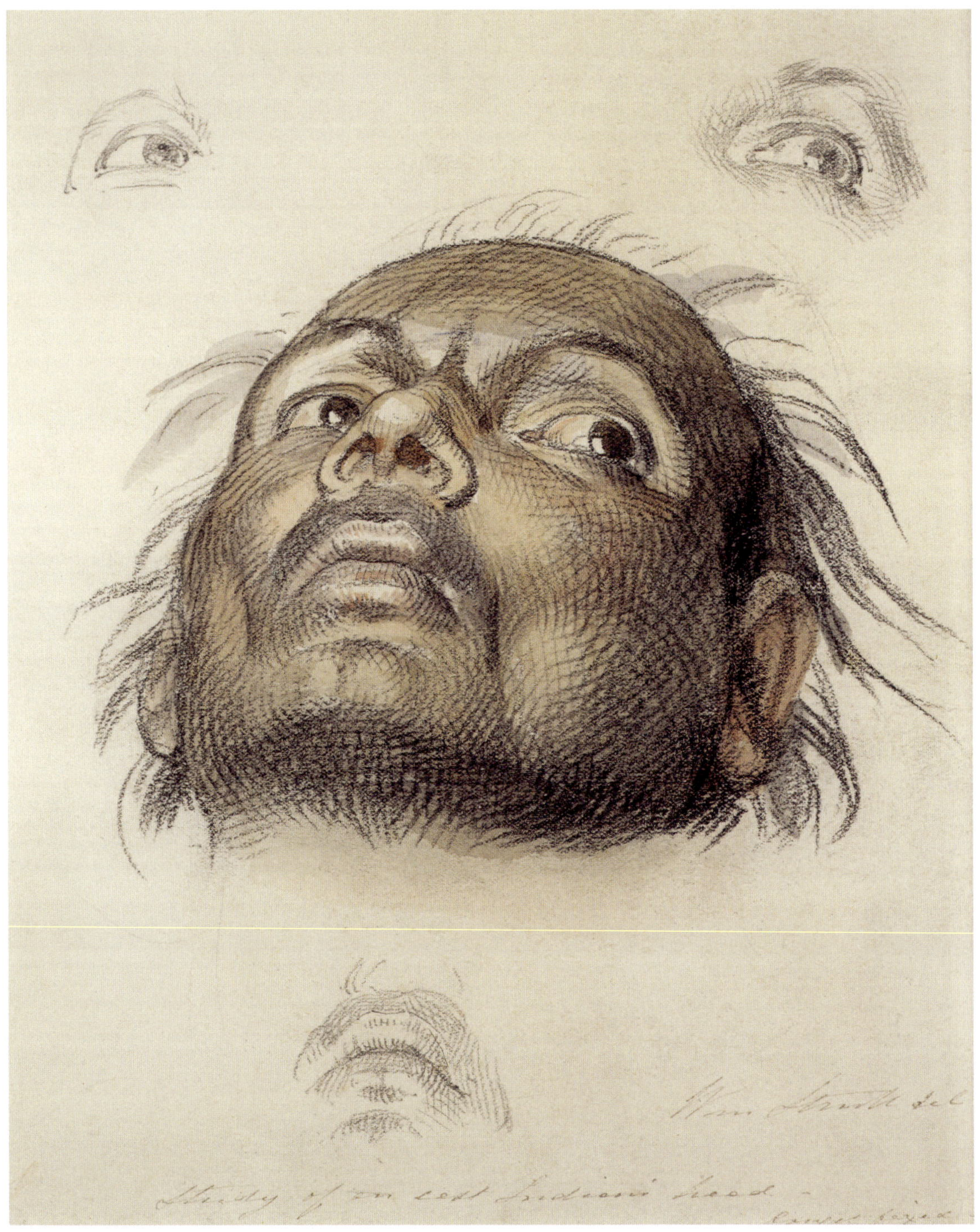

William Strutt
(1825–1915)
STUDY OF AN EAST
INDIAN'S HEAD
C.1875
Crayon and
wash on paper
Private Collection
© Michael Graham-Stewart/
Bridgeman Images

You can show the curve and shiny surface of the eyeball by drawing a small, white, kidney bean shape, to indicate light reflecting off it. This will add realism and help bring your subject to life.

It is the prince of mathematics . . . it has created
architecture, and perspective, and divine painting . . . The
eye is the window of the human body through which the
soul views and enjoys the beauties of the world.
LEONARDO DA VINCI

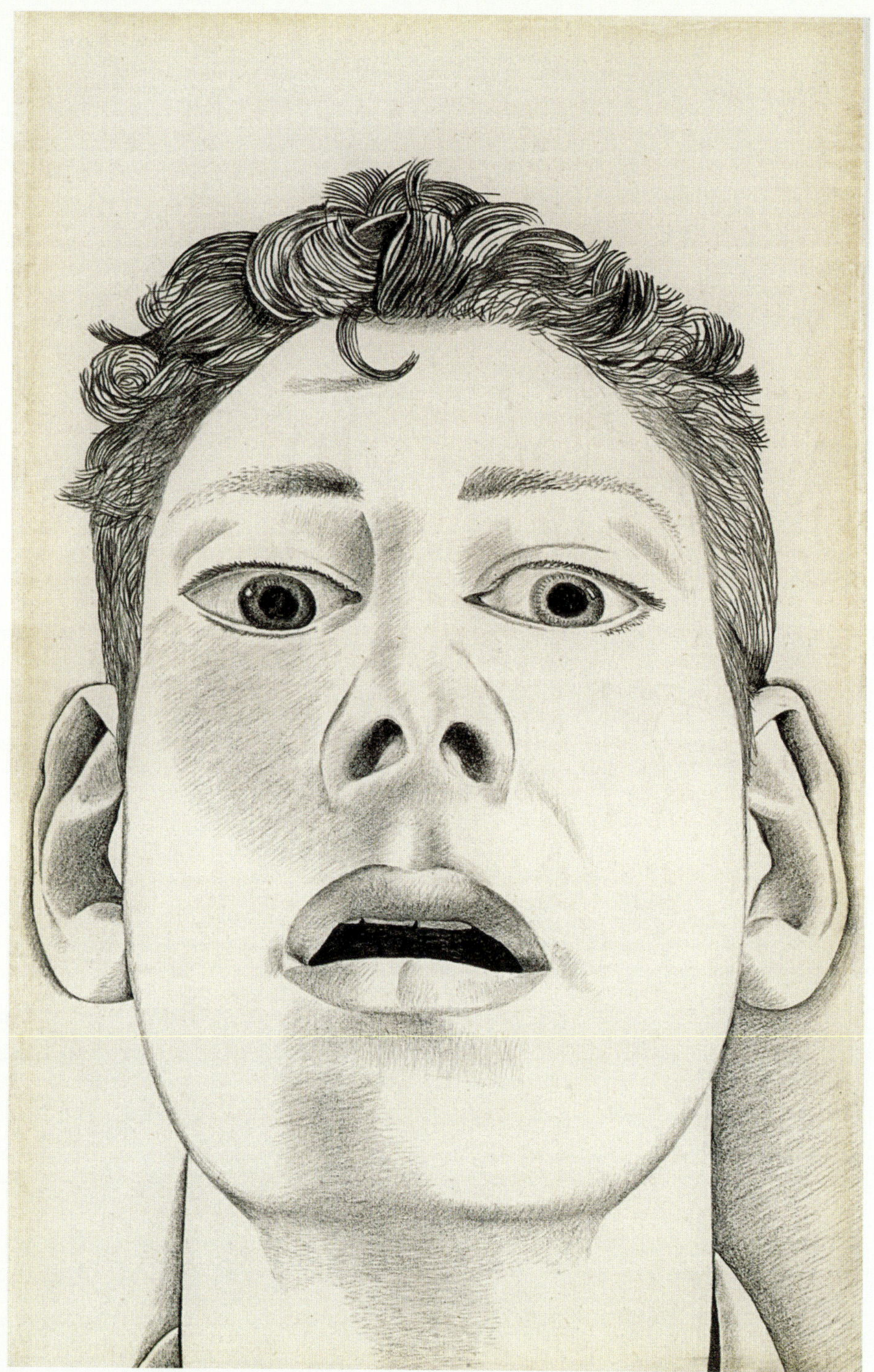

Lucian Freud
(1922—2011)
STARTLED MAN:
SELF PORTRAIT
1948
Pencil on paper
Private Collection/
Bridgeman Images ©
The Lucian Freud Archive

Freud's fleshy, parted lips contribute much to his surprised
expression. The highlighted lips surrounding the cavernous
black shape of the mouth, and dramatic use of perspective,
draw the viewer in while at the same time emphasizing how
the subject appears to be pulling away from us.

The mouth is where the portrait painter finds his true humility.
ROBERT GENN

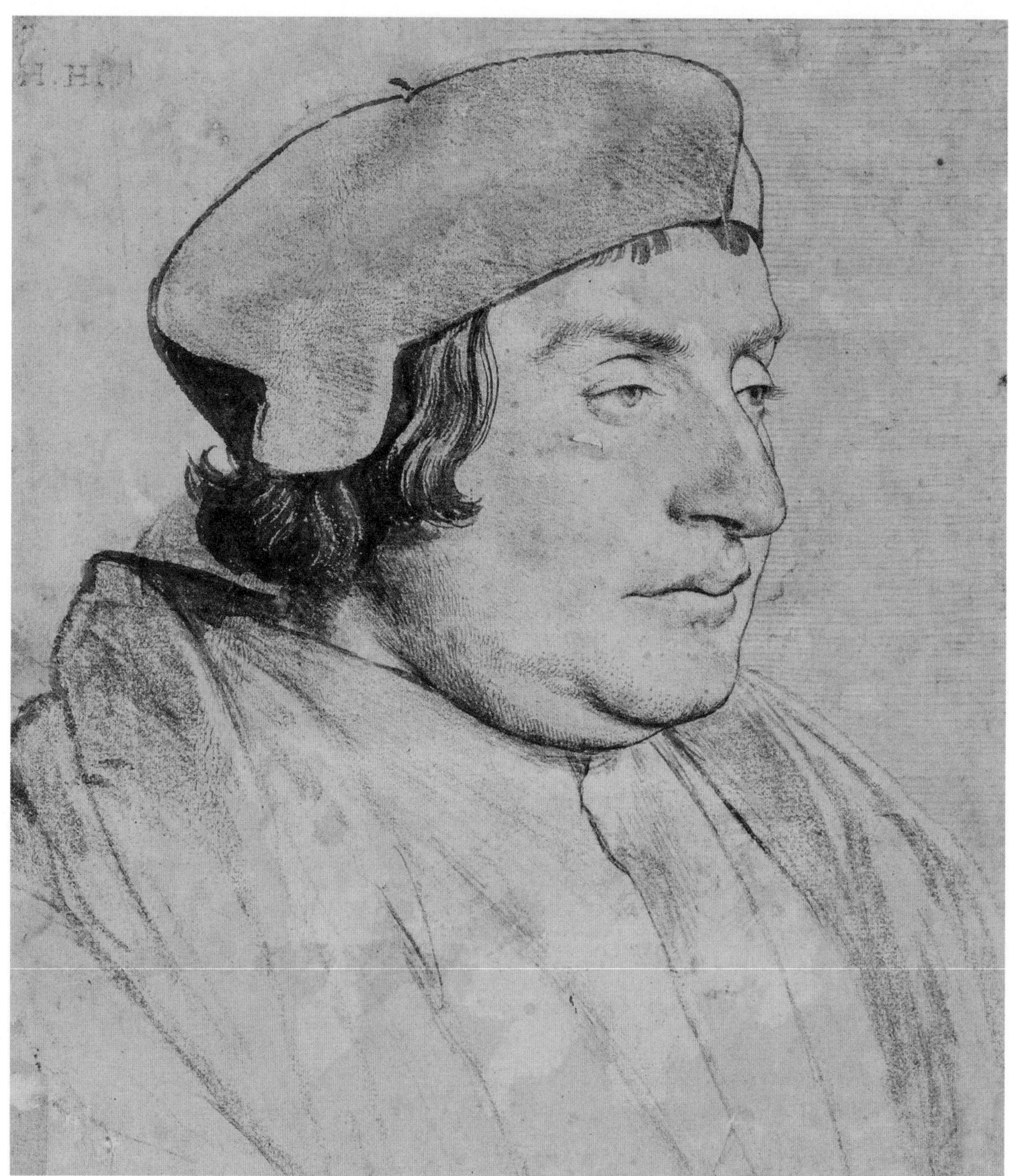

**Hans Holbein
the Younger**

(1497/1498–1543)
PORTRAIT OF
A SCHOLAR
OR CLERIC
1532–1535
Black and red chalk, pen
and brush and black ink
on pink prepared paper

*J. Paul Getty Museum,
California. Image courtesy
of the Getty's Open
Content Program*

Think of the nose as an upside-down comma shape:
follow the bridge to its tip and note how it curves
around to meet the septum and how the wings
curl around to form the nostrils.

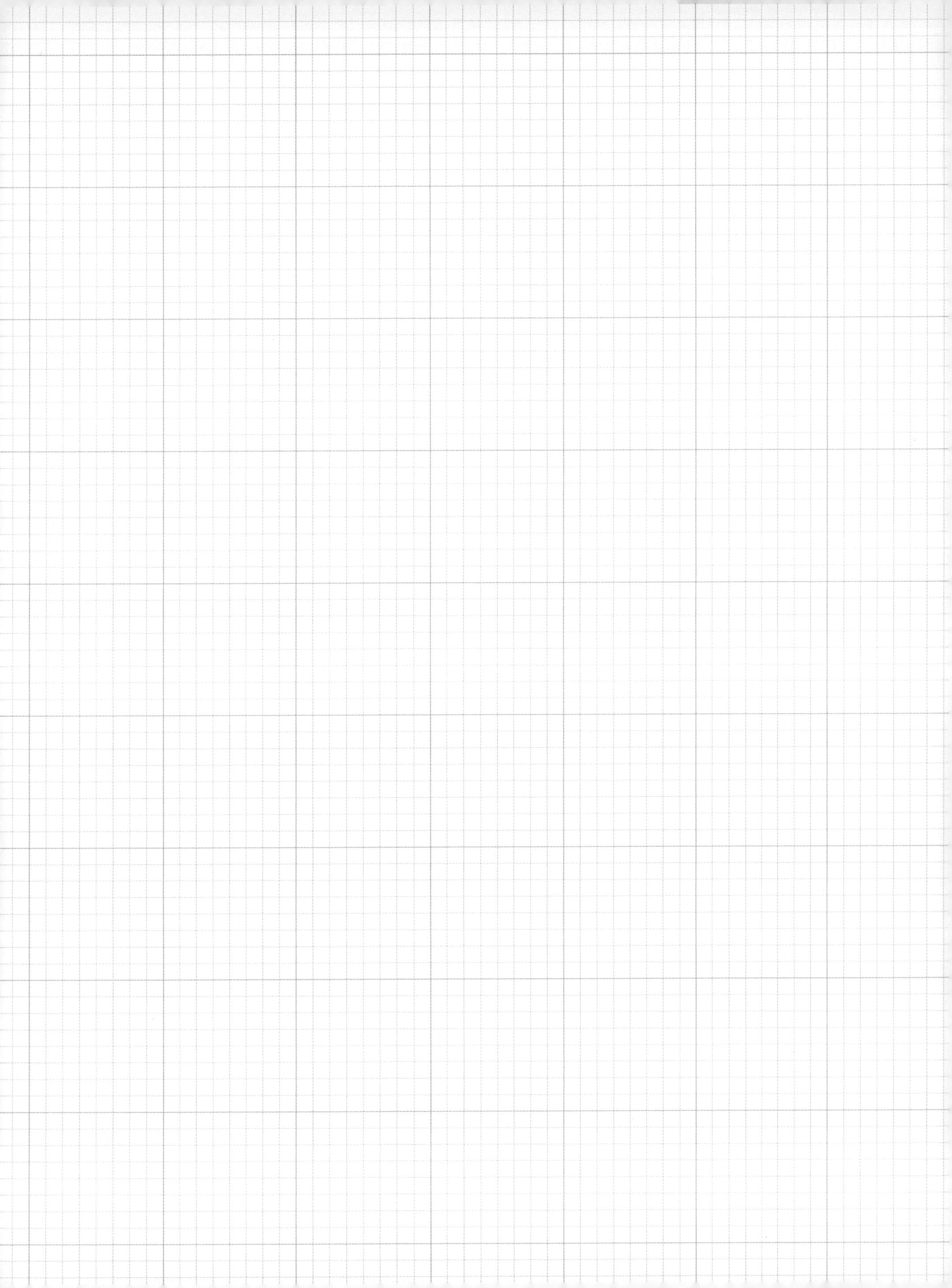

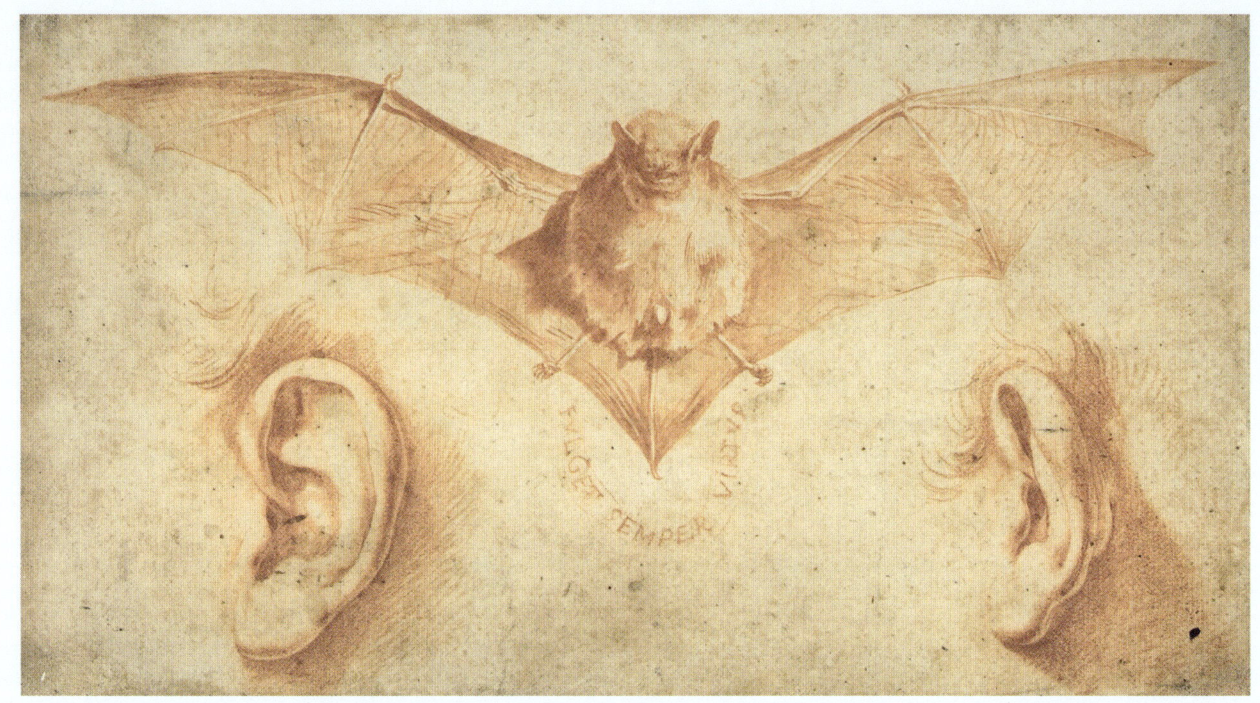

Jusepe de Ribera (called Lo Spagnoletto)
(1591–1652)
STUDIES OF TWO EARS AND OF A BAT
C.1622
Red chalk and brush and red wash on beige paper. Composition outlined on all borders with ruled lines in black chalk

The Metropolitan Museum of Art, New York. Rogers Fund, 1972

Your ears are as unique as your fingerprints. When drawing, take time to study your subject's ear shape—the outer visible part of the ear is a spiral of cartilage also known as the auricle. The earlobe too is particularly distinctive—is your subject's earlobe soft and fleshy, less prominent, or attached to the side of the face?

There is an undeniable difference between Ribera's anatomical
prints and virtually every other example produced in the 17th
century . . . Ribera's drawings of the ear, eye, and nose and
mouth are alive with expression and personality.
JONATHAN BROWN

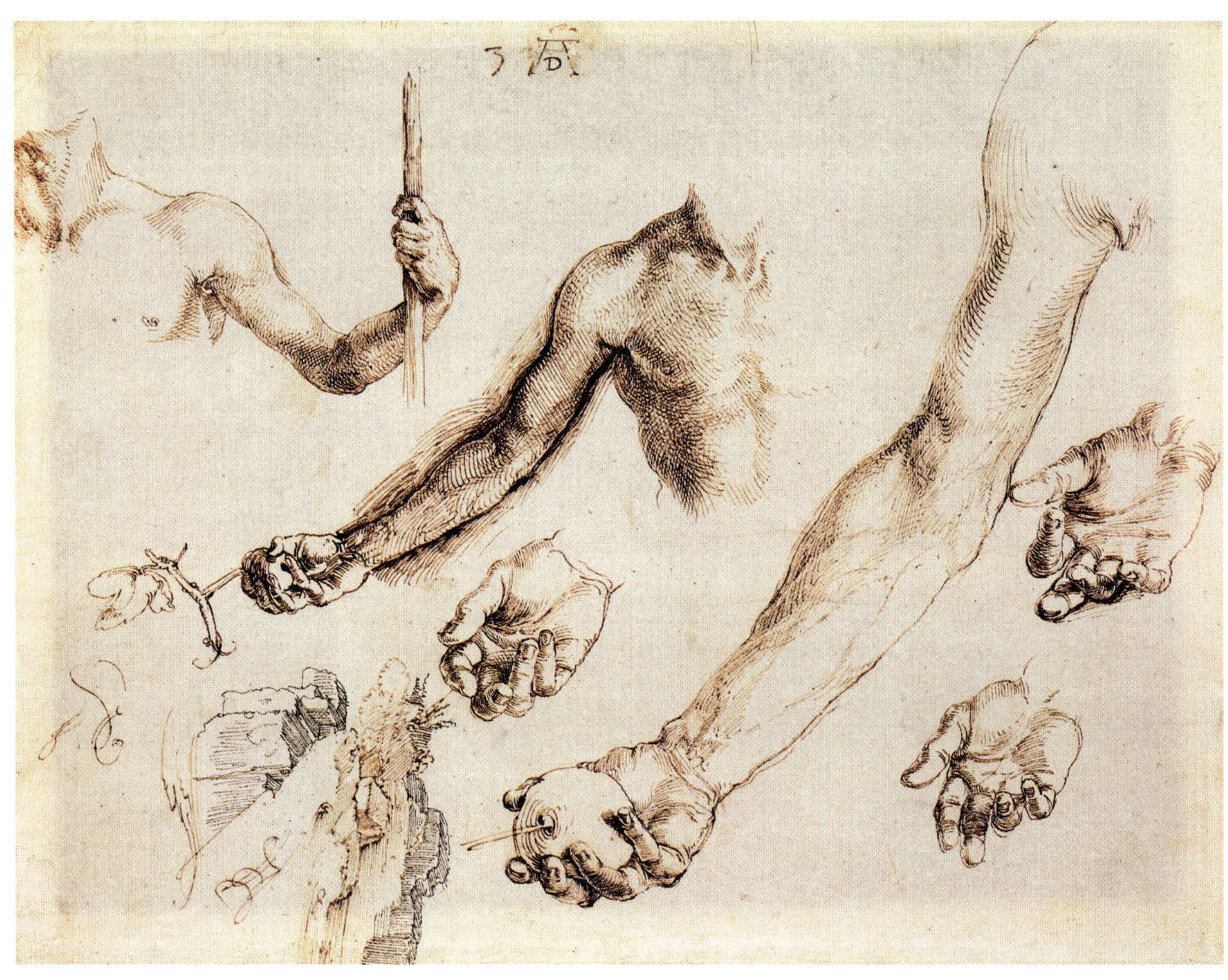

Albrecht Dürer
(1471–1528)
SHEET OF STUDIES
FOR THE HAND AND
ARM OF ADAM AND
FOR ROCKS AND
BUSHES FOR THE
ENGRAVING OF
ADAM AND EVE
1504
Pen and brown and
black ink on paper
British Museum, London/
Bridgeman Images

Proportionally, the upper arm and forearm are the same length. Often you can see arm muscles made taut and visible in poses where the fist is clenched or arm is flexed. Hatching and crosshatching are good for communicating the complex contours of arm muscles, like Dürer does here.

Sane judgment abhors nothing so much as a picture perpetrated with
no technical knowledge, although with plenty of care and diligence.
ALBRECHT DÜRER

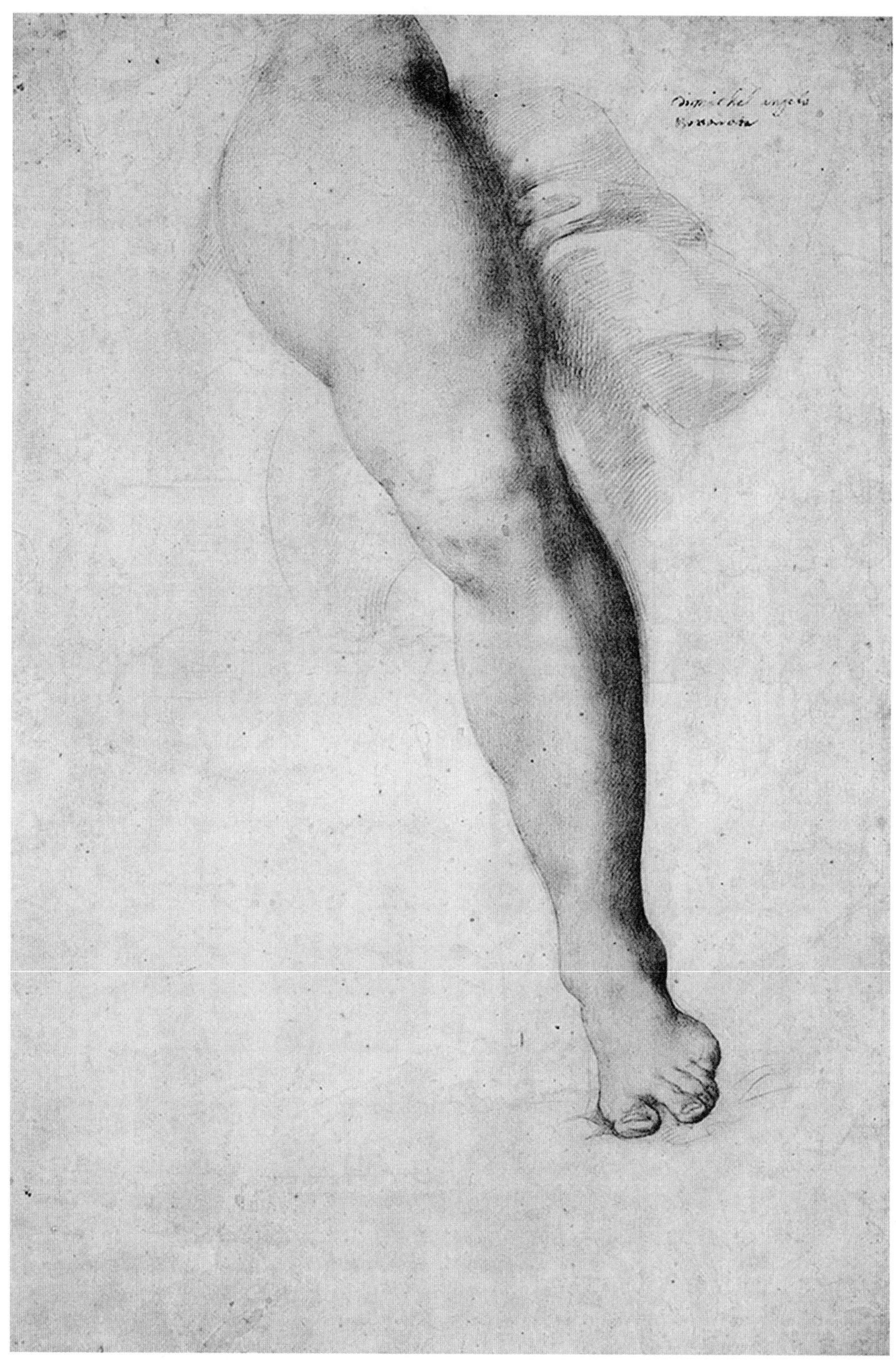

**Bronzino
(Agnolo di Cosimo
di Mariano)**
(1503–1572)
STUDY OF A LEFT
LEG AND DRAPERY
C.1550
Black chalk

*The Metropolitan Museum
of Art, New York. Promised
Gift of David M. Tobey, and
Purchase, several members
of The Chairman's Council
Gifts and Joseph Pulitzer
Bequest, 2006*

A good rule to make sure a figure is in proportion is that the lower limbs should make up half the body height. The fibula, or calf bone, connects the knee and the ankle, and the constant pull of the calf muscles is vital for keeping us upright, and for walking and running.

To draw does not mean simply to reproduce contours;
drawing does not consist merely of line: drawing is also
expression, the inner form, the plane, the modeling.
JEAN-AUGUSTE-DOMINIQUE INGRES

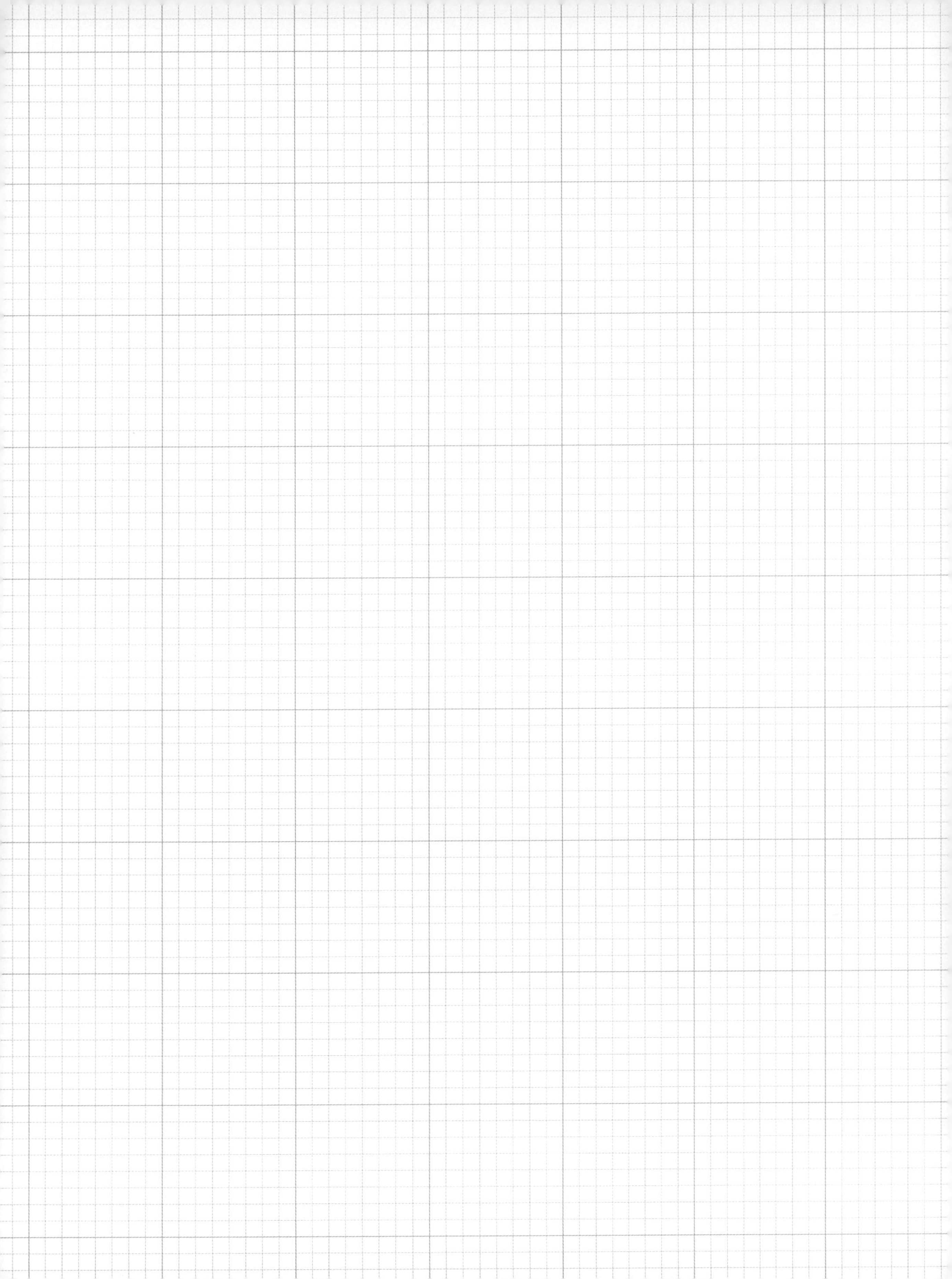

Henry Moore
1898—1986
THE ARTIST'S
LEFT HAND
1980
Ballpoint pen on
white wove paper
Reproduced by permission of
The Henry Moore Foundation

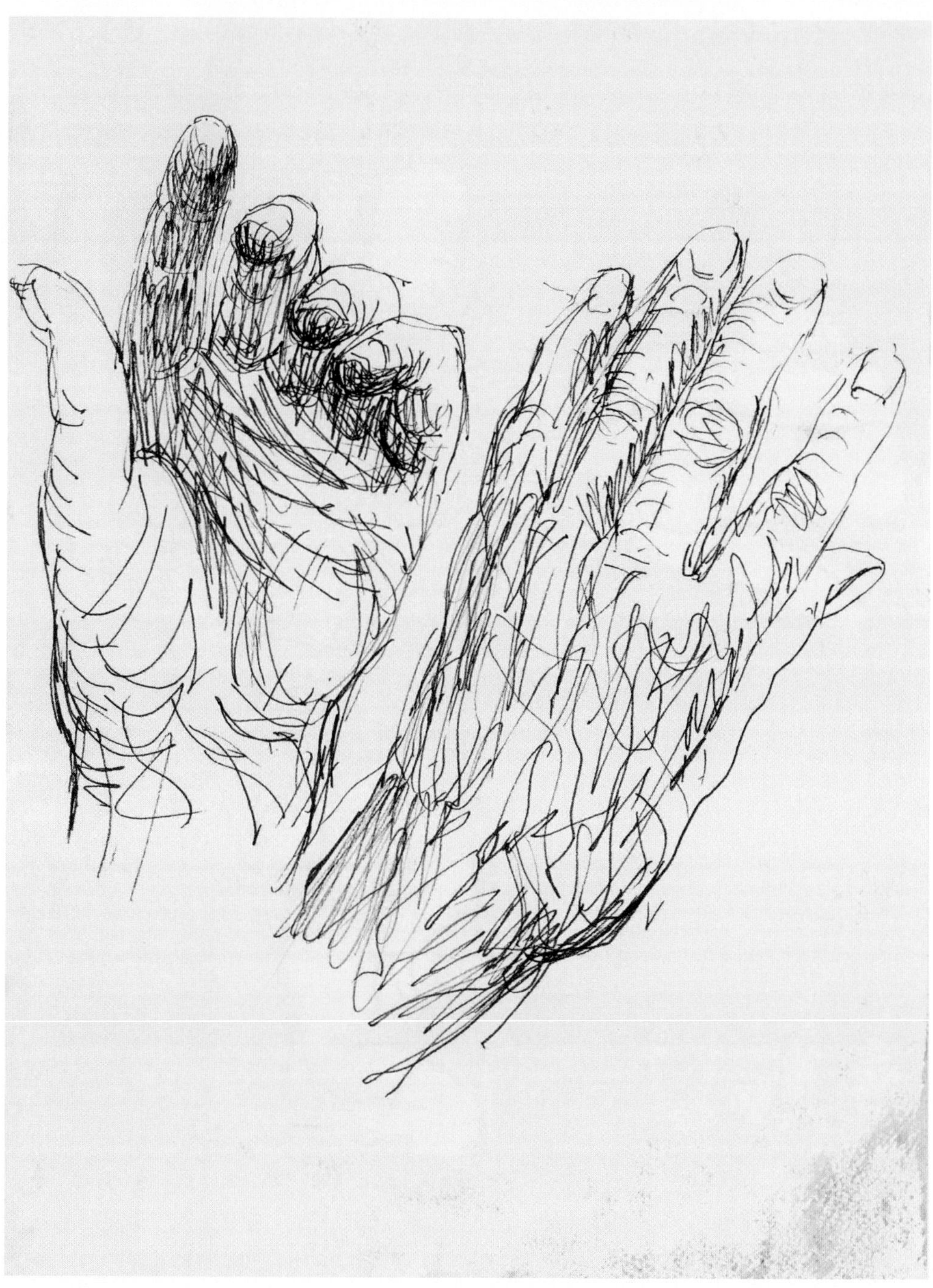

Hands can convey so much——they can beg or refuse . . .
show content or anxiety . . . Throughout the history of
sculpture and painting one can find that artists have shown
through the hands the feelings they wished to represent.
HENRY MOORE

I am not what I am, I am what I do with my hands.
LOUISE BOURGEOIS

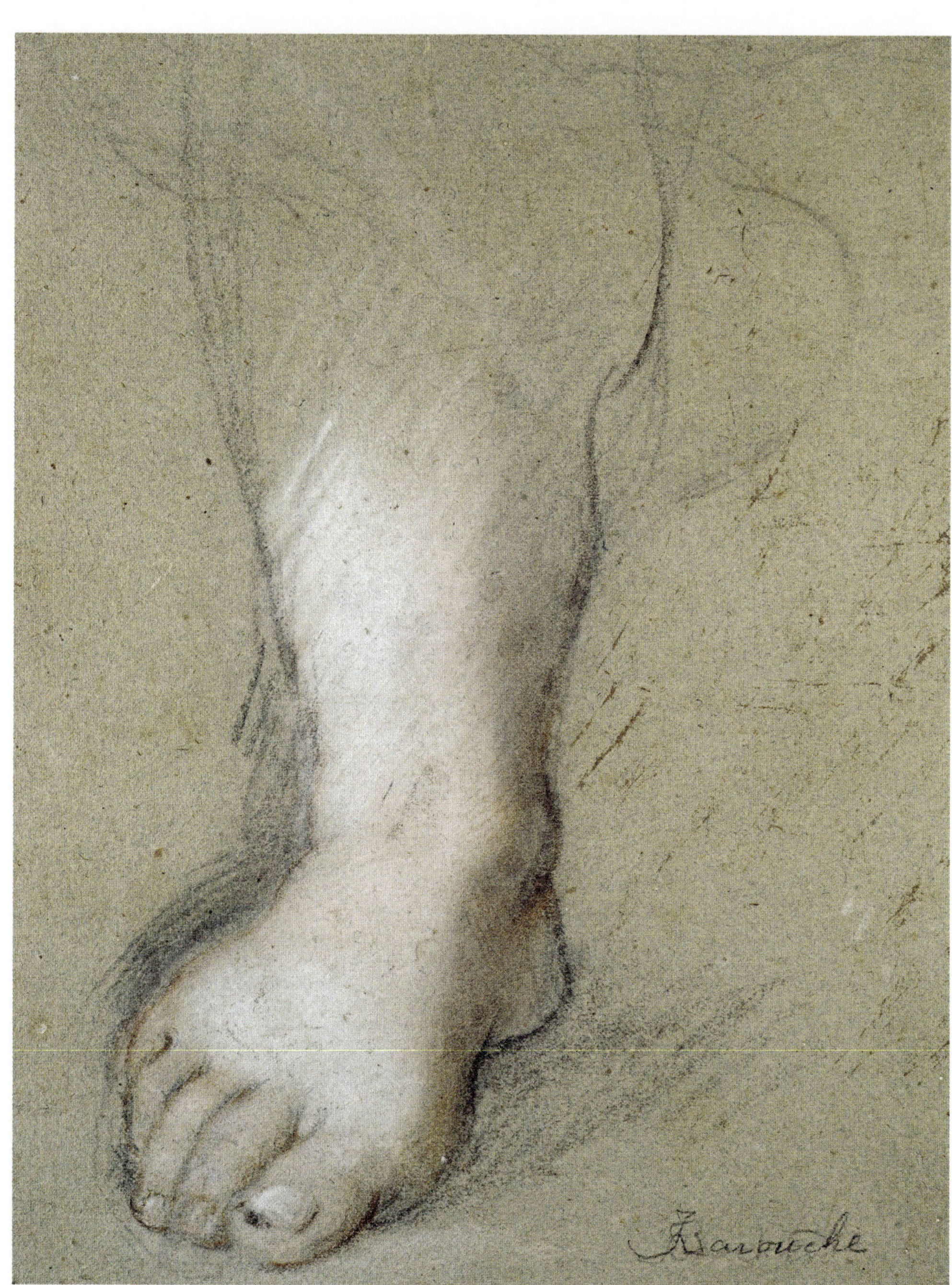

Federico Barocci
(c.1535–1612)
STUDY OF A FOOT
16TH CENTURY
Black, red, pink,
and white chalks
on a grayish paper
*Ashmolean Museum,
University of Oxford/
Bridgeman Images*

Barocci's use of carefully placed highlights and shading
makes a convincing depiction of a foot appear from
a few lines out of nothing. Together with his use of
foreshortening, he gives the illusion of depth, as if
the foot stands out from the page toward us.

There is no excellent beauty, that hath not some strangeness in the proportion.
FRANCIS BACON

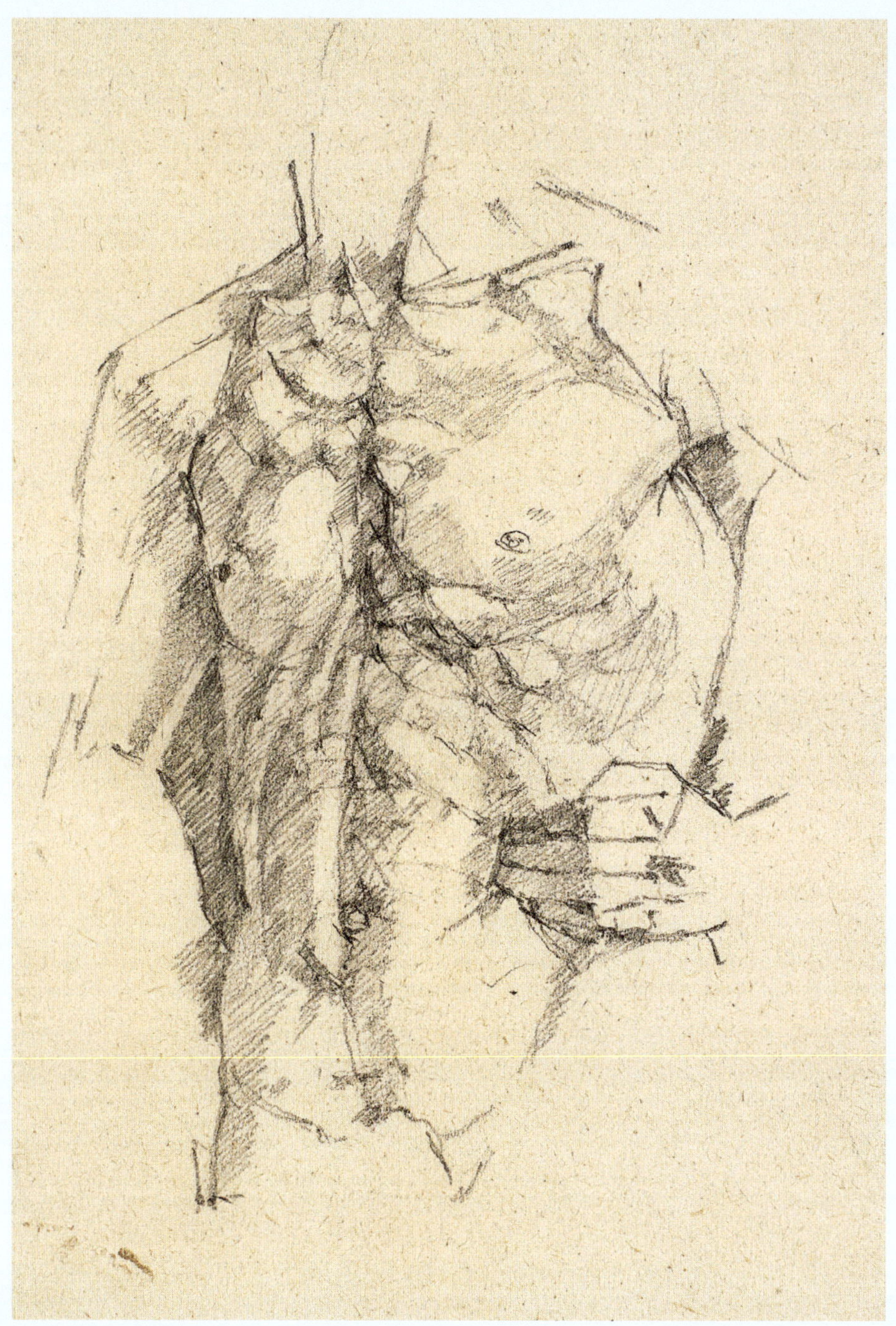

Alberto Giacometti
(1901–1966)
TORSO OF A MAN
C.1922–1925
Pencil on paper
*Collection Fondation Alberto
& Annette Giacometti/
Bridgeman Images © The
Estate of Alberto Giacometti
(Fondation Giacometti,
Paris and ADAGP, Paris),
licenced in the UK by ACS
and DACS, London 2018*

This torso is almost cubist in its treatment. Comprising facets,
it is as though the rib cage of this thin male model is made visible.
The geometric effect is further emphasized by the central bone that
runs through the rib cage and deep V-like structure of the torso.

*When I make my drawings . . . the path traced by my pencil on the sheet of paper is,
to some extent, analogous to the gesture of a man groping his way in the darkness.*
ALBERTO GIACOMETTI

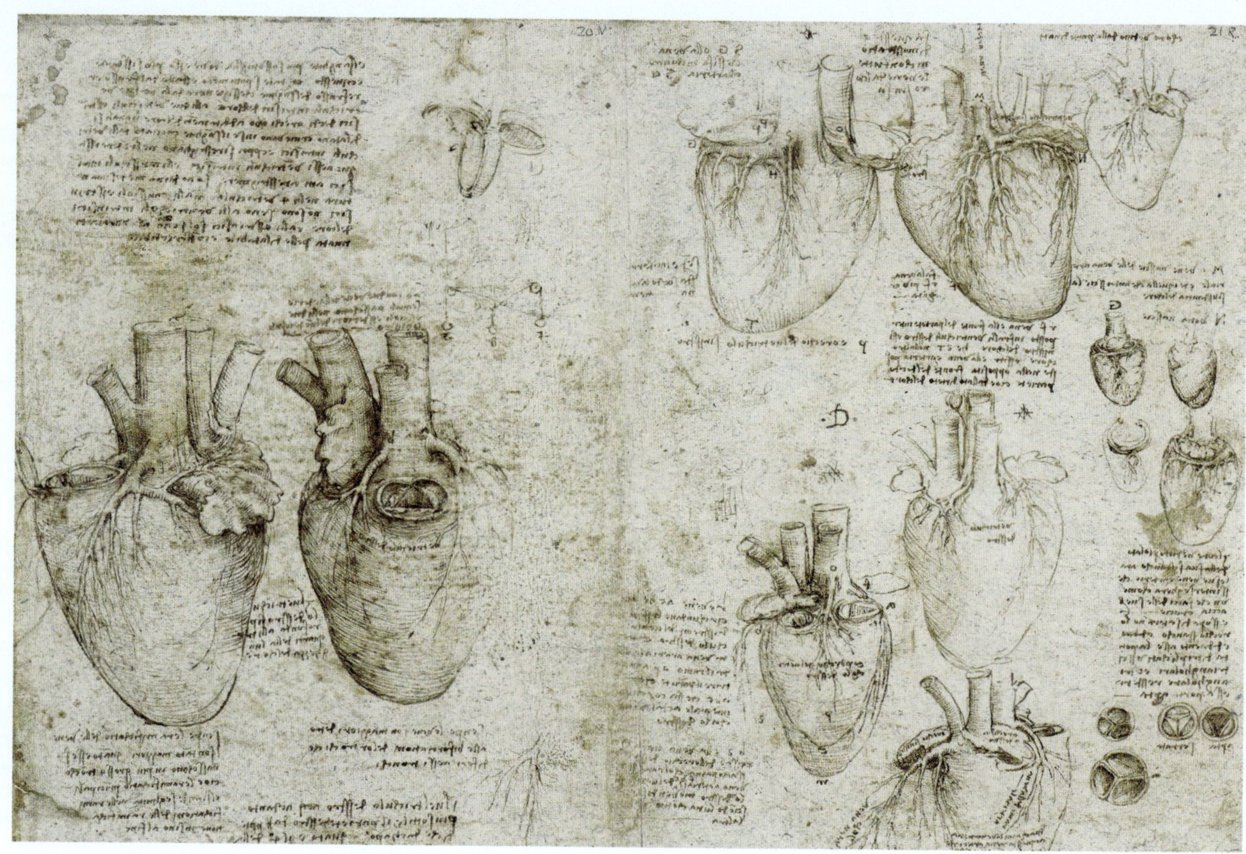

Leonardo da Vinci

(1452–1519)
STUDIES OF
AN OX HEART

C.1512

Pen and ink

Royal Collection Trust © Her Majesty Queen Elizabeth II, 2018/Bridgeman Images

Da Vinci drew thousands of renditions of human anatomy that prove he was centuries ahead of his time in his understanding of the body. It was difficult for him to access human hearts to study until later in his life, so he also studied ox hearts, which are almost identical in structure to human ones.

The heart is roughly conical in shape and made up of four
chambers—the upper left and right atria and the lower
left and right ventricles. In terms of proportion, an adult
heart is about the same size as two adult fists, and a child's
heart is about the same size as one child's fist.

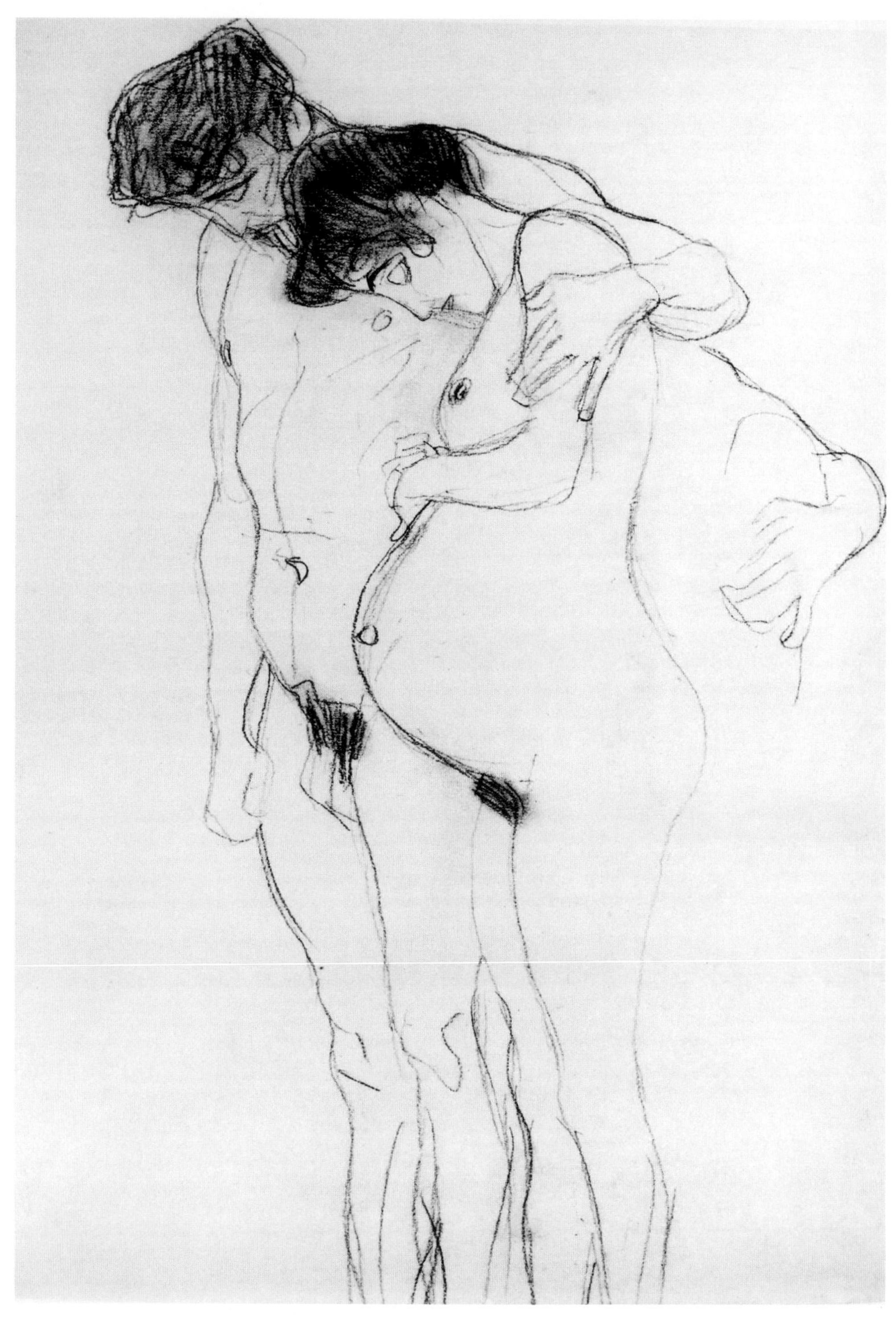

Gustav Klimt
(1862–1918)
STUDY FOR
HOFFNUNG I
(*HOPE I*)
1903–1904
Chalk on paper
Private Collection/
Bridgeman Images

Everything in this drawing brings attention to its focal point: the child-to-be. A pregnant woman is posed in profile. Her hand rests on her bump, emphasizing its spherical shape. We follow the couple's gaze to the stomach and are inspired to think hopefully to the future.

The linea nigra is a dark, brownish line that develops
during pregnancy. It runs down the abdomen through the
navel to the pubic bone. The line is thought to be related
to hormonal changes and darkens with each trimester.

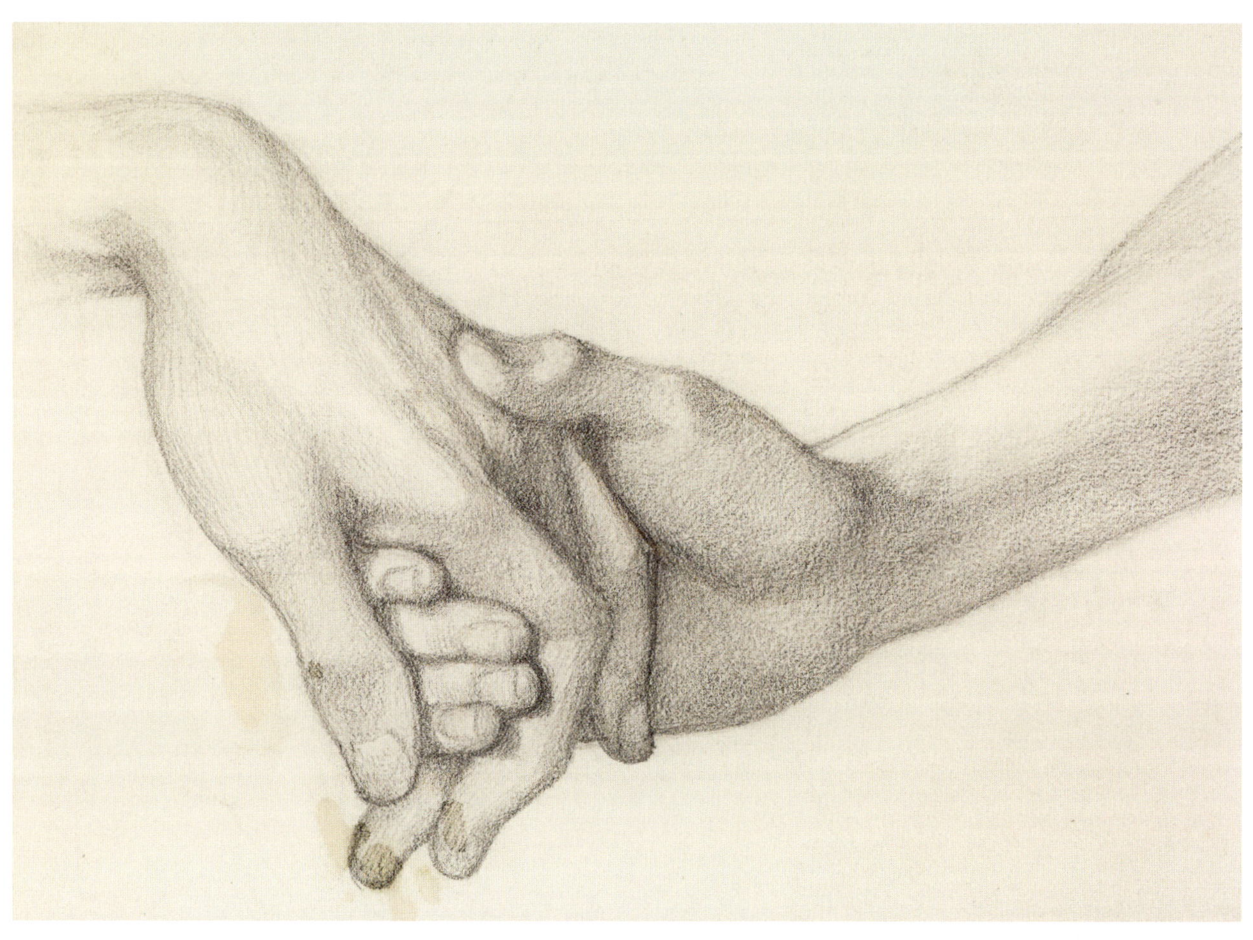

Dante Gabriel
Rossetti
(1828–1882)
STUDY FOR
THE HAND OF
DANTE HOLDING
THAT OF LOVE
1855–1856
Pencil on paper
Birmingham Museums and Art
Gallery/Bridgeman Images

Touch is one of the body's five key senses. We might feel tingling, irritation, pressure—all through the activation of our neural sensors. The simple gesture of holding hands suggests intimacy, dependence, and is also a tactile experience for the viewer.

*The body is the root of all our experience, through
it all our impressions of the world come and from it
all we have to share with the world is expressed.*
ANTONY GORMLEY

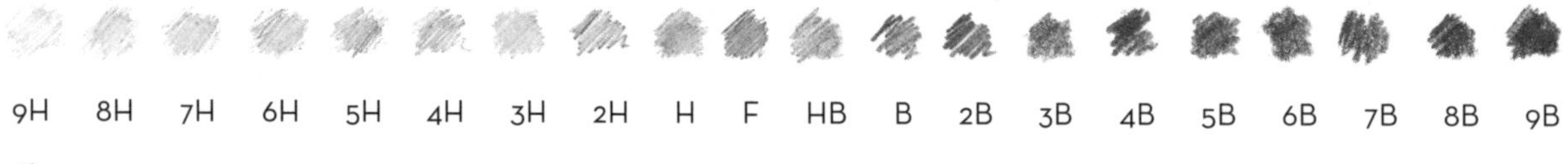

GRAPHITE OR LEAD PENCILS. These are graded from the hardest 9H (H for hard) up to the softest 9B (B for black), with HB (hard black) and F (fine) halfway in between. Soft pencils give a dense, black mark, while hard pencils give a gray mark. If you require a darker mark, do not apply more pressure, but switch to a softer pencil instead.

MECHANICAL PENCILS. These pencils can be extended as necessary without the need for constant sharpening.

WATER-SOLUBLE GRAPHITE PENCILS. These are available in a range of grades, and can be used dry, dipped in water, or the strokes worked into with a wet brush to create watercolor-like effects. They offer the versatility of combining linear marks with tonal washes.

GRAPHITE STICKS. Graphite sticks have a soft texture that makes them suited to large, bold drawings. Available in various sizes and grades, you can also buy them as irregular shaped chunks and as fine graphite powder that can be applied to textured paper.

CHARCOAL. This is the oldest drawing medium, dating from prehistoric times. It comes in different lengths and thicknesses, as well as chunks for especially expressive drawings. Stick charcoal, being brittle and powdery, is ideal for broad areas of tone. Compressed charcoal is made from charcoal dust and clay pressed into shape, and tends to be harder than stick charcoal, making it useful for more detailed, linear work. Charcoal pencils use compressed charcoal.

INKS. There are two main types of ink used by artists. Waterproof ink can be diluted with water and becomes permanent when dry, so line work can be overlaid with washes without smudging. Water-soluble ink, on the other hand, can be blended with water, or reworked with water when dry if corrections are needed.

DIP PENS AND NIBS. Nibs on dip pens can make lines of varying widths depending on the amount of pressure applied, or the back of the nib can be used to make broader marks. Dip pens do have to be reloaded with ink with each stroke, however, to get consistent marks.

SKETCHING PENS, FOUNTAIN PENS, AND TECHNICAL PENS. These are ideal sketching tools, enabling you to use ink on location without having to carry bottles of ink around.

ROLLERBALL, FIBER-TIP, AND MARKER PENS. These are good for sketching out ideas and come in a wide range of colors, but can lack variation in line width individually, although they are available in various sizes.

COLORED PENCILS. Colored pencils contain a colored pigment mixed with clay and coated with wax so that there is no need for a fixative when using them, as they do not smudge easily. Huge color ranges are available, but this is necessary as they cannot be physically blended together to create new shades.

WATER-SOLUBLE PENCILS. These can be used to make conventional pencil drawings but the strokes made with water-soluble pencils can also be worked into with water to create watercolor effects.

CONTÉ PENCILS AND CRAYONS. These are made from pigment and clay and are available either bound in wood to make pencils or as small square sticks. They are softer and less waxy than ordinary colored pencils, but not as soft and crumbly as pastels.

PASTELS. Pastels are exceptionally versatile and ideal for producing quick sketches where a bold effect is desired. They are available in hard and soft forms, but cannot be mixed physically to create new colors. Instead they have to be blended by overlapping strokes on the paper, hence there are many varieties of boxed sets in assorted colors.

OIL PASTELS. These pastels have an added binder of oil so they are not as crumbly as pure pastels and also smudge less. They have the thick, buttery quality of oil paints, and are good for bold, confident strokes. They respond like oil paints, and oil pastel drawings can be worked with a brush dipped in turpentine to achieve a wash effect or scratched into using a sgraffito technique.

PASTEL PENCILS. These have strong colors and the pencil shape makes them ideal for more detailed linear work.

PAPERS. The color, texture, and quality of the paper will play an important part in your finished picture. Dry media that is worked loosely and lightly will result in the color of the paper showing through. Pastels and charcoal will require a paper with enough texture to hold the powder, whereas conté pencils can be used on smoother grades of paper. The most common drawing paper has a smooth surface that is suitable for graphite, colored pencil, and ink work.

LARGE SOFT BRUSH. This is useful for brushing away excess dust when working with powdery media.

FIXATIVE. As charcoal, pastels, and other powdery media smudge easily, finished drawings made in these media should be sprayed with a fixative to bind the powder particles to the paper surface.

SHARPENER, SCALPEL, OR CRAFT KNIFE. These are needed to sharpen the points of pencils and pastel sticks.

TORCHON (stump of rolled paper). A torchon is useful for blending pastel colors and charcoal, though a rag or cotton swab will work too.

ERASERS. Kneaded or putty erasers are the most useful, as small pieces can be rolled off and shaped however you wish for subtle, precise erasing.

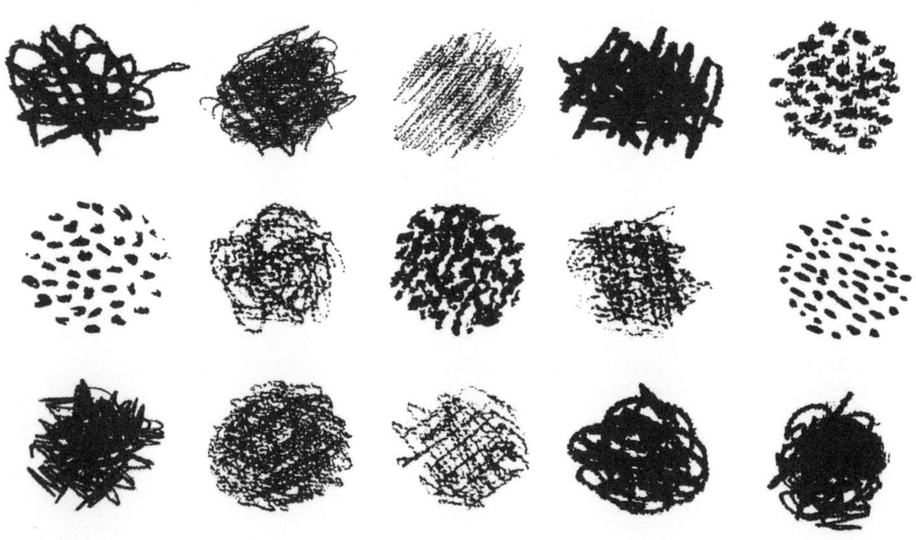

TECHNIQUES —

COLOR BLENDING. Use your finger, a torchon, a brush, or a piece of tissue to blend colors together smoothly on the paper.

SOFT BLENDING. This technique is ideally used with charcoal. As charcoal is a soft medium, you can blend it with your finger to create a smooth, velvety effect.

SCUMBLING. This is a term used to describe the technique of mixing colors optically by laying one color lightly over another. The area where the two colors overlap will give the illusion of a third color.

LINEAR STROKES. This technique is particularly useful for pastel sticks. Using a pastel stick on its widest side will achieve broad bands of color, running the tip or edge of the stick down the paper will produce thin lines, and using the flat end of the pastel will produce bands of color as thick as the pastel.

HATCHING. This is a technique where parallel lines are used to suggest tone and color. By varying the weight and density of the hatched lines, tonal variation can quickly be achieved to great effect. Looser, scribbled lines give a sketchier look.

CROSSHATCHING. This is a development of hatching to indicate differences in shade, where two or more sets of parallel lines are combined, one set crossing another at an angle. The lines can be crosshatched at any angle, or even curved to follow along shapes, and the density varied. However it is a labor-intensive technique.

POINTILLISM. This is a way of building up an area with small dots. By increasing the density of the dots you can increase the density of the color and shading effect. From a distance, dots that are more closely spaced will appear to merge in one mass of color even if they are not touching.

TONE. Tone is built up through a series of loose strokes. To practice, draw a small rectangle and fill it in slowly with strokes, increasing the density to achieve darker tones.

HIGHLIGHTS. These can be picked out in areas of tone by using a kneadable putty eraser or a stick of white chalk. Chalk will deliver sharper, cleaner highlights whereas a putty eraser is subtler.

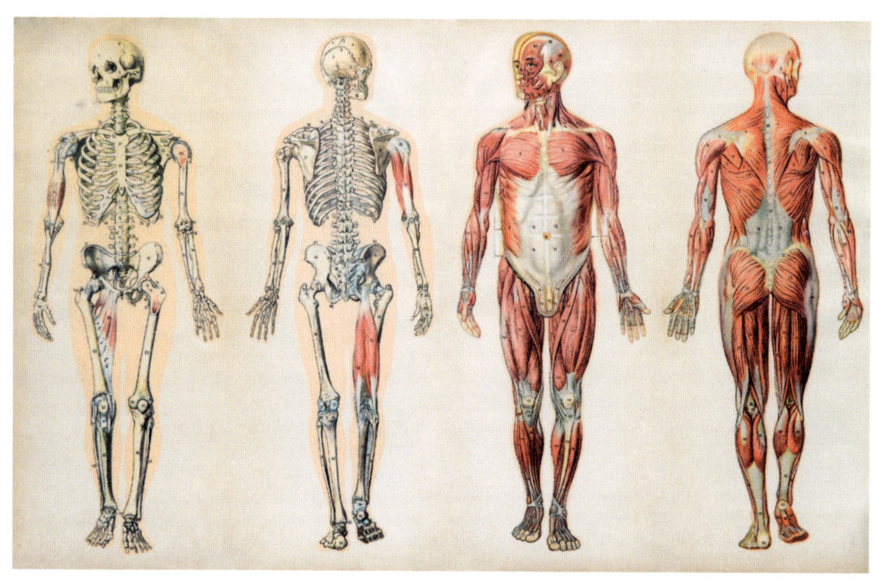

ANATOMY, MEASURING, AND PROPORTIONS —
BASIC ANATOMY

Before perfecting the details of what you see, think about how the body is behaving; what hangs beneath the surface of the skin and why it makes the body shape that you can see. While you may not have an anatomical model to draw from, a basic understanding of anatomy will help you to depict the human body, and especially its tones, more accurately. It is a good idea to have an understanding of the body's structural sections—head, spine, rib cage, shoulders, arms and hands, pelvis, legs and feet—as well as the typical differences between the male and female figures. As you draw, consider some of the bones you may see protruding, the muscles that hold together the bones, and how the movement, prominence, and tension of these muscles define the figure before you.

MEASURING

Even the most proficient artist needs to continually check while working that all the proportions drawn are true to life. If drawing a face, close one eye and holding a pencil at arm's length, measure, for example, the distance from the forehead to the chin, using the tip of your thumb against the pencil as your measurement mark. Transfer this unit of measurement to the paper relative to the scale you are drawing to, for example drawing at double the size of the pencil measurements. You can then use this same scale to measure the other distances of the object, such as the width of the face from ear to ear and so on, so that the ratio will be consistent when applied to the paper.